Lucy Addison was born in Latvia, and lived there all her life. When war broke out, she and her husband refused to leave the country with the rest of the British community, but stayed on to face first the Nazi, then the Russian occupations. Lucy's beloved grand-daughters had been sent home to England, so Lucy wrote to them regularly. When the postal system broke down, she kept a journal. What emerges is a remarkable picture of a country, and of a family, at war.

Rhona Chave was Lucy Addison's grand-daughter.

LETTERS FROM LATVIA

by Lucy Addison
edited by Rhona Chave

Futura

A *Futura* Book

Copyright © Rhona Chave 1986

First published in Great Britain in 1986 by
Macdonald & Co (Publishers) Ltd
London & Sydney

This edition published in 1987 by
Futura Publications, a Division of
Macdonald & Co (Publishers) Ltd
London & Sydney

ISBN 0 7088 3259 8

Printed and bound in Great Britain by
The Guernsey Press Co. Ltd, Guernsey, Channel Islands.

Futura Publications
A Division of
Macdonald & Co (Publishers) Ltd
Greater London House
Hampstead Road
London NW1 7QX

A BPCC plc Company

For my family,
and in memory of a life that is gone

INTRODUCTION

My family had lived and worked in Latvia since an ancestor went to Riga during the Napoleonic Wars to help provide the timber that the British Navy needed for the vast wooden fleet that then dominated the oceans. Lucy Addison, my grandmother, had come out from England to marry my grandfather, but her own family had strong Baltic connections. I grew up in a multi-lingual, culturally cosmopolitan society. Now it would perhaps be thought of as complacent and insular. Then, it seemed just natural, though we all knew, if we didn't admit it, that it was privileged.

For me, looking back over five decades, this life we lived then was a Paradise. I suppose that there were bad days, bad times, but in my memory it is always summer. There were houses, there were parties, there was a warm and loving family atmosphere. I never imagined that it could end. But of course it did. When Stalin and Hitler signed their infamous pact in 1939, the writing was on the wall, and I was sent away to England, never to return.

Latvia is a small country, hardly known beyond its borders. The inhabitants are an interesting racial mix: Letts, who have always been there; and Balts, a people of German origins who have been established there for centuries, but who have always had a certain alien quality — something, I suppose, like the Protestants in Northern Ireland, or the Flemmings in Belgium. There was always an internal rivalry — I remember that the small English community took it for granted and indeed laughed about it. (Independence came late to Latvia, which had been dominated by Russia since the eighteenth century, and we were, in retrospect, condescending to a degree!) It was the First World War and the Revolution that allowed a Latvian Republic to come into being. With independence, and a new urgency to political life, the differences between Letts and Balts took on a new significance, a political importance which, though real, was not a matter for bitterness. In the end, it was Hitler, and his determination to unite Germans, whether they liked it or not, who made that difference a matter, very literally, of life and death. For he forcibly 'repatriated' the often very reluctant Balts to a most uncertain future in Greater Germany — and much of Latvian life and businesses came to a grinding halt. Personally, I was never really aware of any problems — I suppose the small but close-knit and very prosperous English community, most of whom, like my own family, had been in Latvia for generations, but, though of the community, were *apart* from it, paid very little attention. Their loyalty, often very sentimental, was to Home (the Union Jacks which decorated our house for my sister's wedding in 1938 were typical — and incidentally a source of amusement and even pride, to our Latvian neighbours).

When in 1939 my world, as it was then, came to an end, and I was sent away to England, never to see my grandparents, my father or my aunt again, it was a close-knit and deeply affectionate tribe that I was leaving. Lucy my grandmother, already in her late seventies, Ganf, my grandfather, two years older, but in my memory forever young, Noony, my aunt, and my father, were deeply devoted to each other, and to me and to my sister Lorna.

It is this devotion — the separation imposed by the war was a wound that to this day has never really healed — that led to the letters, and the journal, which Mumsy wrote for both of us, her grandchildren, so that we could share life with her, and could remember, keep track of, the Latvia we had left behind. Of course, none of us could know that we would never meet again. Somehow that adds a poignancy to Mumsy's letters which she, no sentimentalist, would find distasteful. I don't think she would approve at all of this collection, though I have tried to be as true to her as memory allows.

At first, the mail came through, if often irregularly. The Russians came — and then the Germans. And the Russians again. When all contact was lost, my grandmother kept a journal — two, in fact, one for me and one for Lorna. Finally contact was restored, and it was letters again, whole bundles of them. It is extraordinary that through all the privations, the almost unendurable difficulties, my grandmother had the energy

8

to maintain contact with her grandchildren. She was truly a woman of extraordinary energy, the sort of Englishwoman who helped to make, and to rule, an Empire. She was a woman of her time, often intolerant, often difficult, certainly strong-willed, never one to be overlooked. But despite, for instance, the anti-semitism which was then so much a part of upper middle-class life, when confronted with the practicalities of Nazi rule, she could, and did, set that aside, without regret. She believed in people. All her life she had taught, both English and music, and her approach was a practical one. Whatever the theory, people were people, and commonsense, her abiding passion, would lead her on crusade, if necessary. This is her monument, which she would not have sought, but which she, and thousands like her, richly deserve. I hope that this portrait of a family at war will help to keep at least one small but vital memory alive.

Rhona Chave

PART

1

Saturday   Bulduri
                                     September 16th 1939

My darling Rhona

It was a great joy and relief to receive your wire yesterday
morning. Thank God your perilous journey is safely over.
Many thanks for your post cards from Tallinu, S'holm and
Oslo. It was thoughtful of you to write. We heard from Aunt
Alice today, and though the letter was thirteen days old, it gives
us hope that our correspondence will trickle through sometimes. As soon as you had left I locked the door of your room
and the next day I cleaned your looking glass cupboard and put
away all your possessions and firmly locked them up, so that
when you come home you will find everything intact. We have
had a bumper harvest from our three little apple trees. All the
available tables are covered with apples and there is a huge
heap on the floor; there are at the very least 1000, and nearly
as many again on the trees. I sent a big basketful to Daddy,
because he has very few this year.

Sophka* is still here. We have not seen fur or feather of
the Maiers. Everybody we know has left the Strand, and the
season is over; but Nooney continues to bathe in the sea.
Dorriecorrie is coming for the week-end.

The white room being full of apples and later on of
flowers etc, I have turned *your* room into a schoolroom; up till
now I have very few lessons, but I hope for more, as my
mornings are quite free.

God bless you, my Treasure.

Tenderest love and kisses from
Your devoted, loving
Mumsy

Lucy Addison

* Rhona's pony

13

Monday

My darling Rhona

I was surprised this morning to see the ground and the roofs covered with snow — awfully early for winter to set in. Last night there were torrents of rain, it was bitterly cold, and it turned into snow. It looks odd with the leaves still in full leaf, and the sun shining brightly. Mrs Maier sent for your gee-gee on Saturday. It was sad to see her go, and I hope she will find a good home. She was fetched very opportunely, as she had just kicked her door to pieces — for want of exercise, I suppose. She had been happily grazing latterly, tethered to a tree. We have received your little powder-box which you left at Stockholm. It came in the bag and I have put it in your cupboard with the rest of your belongings.

Grandfather (Ganf) now takes a constitutional twice a day; I am terrified lest he should catch cold in this changeable weather. Most people have gone to town, as the schools have begun, and soon we shall be alone in our glory. Dorothy spent the weekend with us. We are all busy sewing garments for the Polish refugees — there are about 1000 of them here — and I am crocheting blankets for the children. No more news.

Ever your devoted, loving Grandmother (Mumsy)

Lucy Addison

Sunday

Bulduri
October 1st 1939

My own darling Rhona

We have heard from the British Consul that you have found a very congenial job and I hope you enjoy it and are well and happy. What a blessing you know Latvian so well.

We are having the double windows put in and the verandah closed in today, as we anticipate an early winter — and so the house will be rather gloomy.

We had an air raid practice the other day. The whole house was in darkness; we sat in the growlery with the shutters up and the curtains drawn — and had to grope our way about the house. Two trains stopped at some distance from the station — as soon as the siren went all the passengers had to jump out and run into the woods. Dorriecorrie said it was awful fun in town. The town was in complete darkness, and the streets absolutely empty. All the people scurrying to take shelter in the Anlagen — bumping up against each in the dark and shrieking with muffled laughter. She had to take a telegram to the P.O. Every time she was stopped by a policeman she said 'valsts telegr', and sped on. Daddy has taken on the job of courier, as there is nothing doing in the factory, so he will be away from home most of the time. I have written to you every Sunday — hope you have received my letters. We have not heard from you since you arrived. I should so like to have your address — God bless you, my darling child.

Your loving Mumsy

Lucy Addison

Not heard from Lorna for two months

Bulduri
October 8th 1939

My own darling Rhona

I hope you have really got the job the Consul's wife told us of, and having got it that you will persevere. The papers will have told about all the astonishing developments here, and today's news says that Hitler has ordered all the Balts to go and live in Germany. Serve them right for grumbling, but I don't think they will find it all beer and skittles. Leaving their houses and property in a land of comparative plenty to go and starve in Germany. Our weather is cold and damp, and I live in terror of Ganf catching cold. He *will* go out twice a day whatever the weather. He goes round by Klara's and back through the wood, and gets home rather breathless.

We have to have sugar-cards and each get 3 lbs of sugar a month — quite enough. In my last I told you that Liesel had sent for your horse, and that I hoped she would have a good home, though she will not like the cobbles as much as the sandy soil. Daddy has undertaken the job of courier, and he is off tomorrow. Lina will feel lonely, because he will be away from home a great deal. Have you read *The Woman at the Door* by Warwick Deeping? It is awfully thrilling. I have just bought it for Pops. I have very few pupils, just seven for the present.

We have a marvellous stove in the kitchen. It burns sawdust and keeps in for ten hours without being replenished. Hot water all day and one can even cook on it. Four loads of sawdust have been dumped in Sophka's stall.

God bless you my Treasure.

Love and a kiss from your loving Mumsy

Lucy Addison

Bulduri
October 14th 1939

Darling Rouite

You will have had several more letters from Mum and me by now with news of Sophie in each of mine; the Maiers drove her in a trap one day and said she went fine — if it gets warm enough to bike to Meza Park I will go to see her one day. The harbour is full of Hun ships waiting to take almost the entire Balt population off — a hospital ship leaves on Monday with *all* the cases from the Vacu Hospital and country hospitals and the old people from all the poor houses. We lose 123 doctors and surgeons including Faust and Kreisler! Eighty chemists from Riga — Hartmann (the second police chief), all those serving in the Army and even the criminals out of the prisons!!! We also lose the whole of the aristocracy and upper classes of the country — only the natives, whose upper classes evolved in the present century, remain.

The Hellmanns, Shuberts, Mershutz, Hermarcks, Rosengreens and every one of the old ladies Mum and I visit, even Frl Schultz — fade away from our ken never to return to the land in which the bones of their remote ancestors lie buried. Nothing like this has happened in the world since the Israelites migrated from Egypt. And none of them know where they are going, 'cept that it is some devastated town in the Corridor. They have been told that their houses and furniture will be valued by a commission and the Letts will sell their property, the money to be paid to a bank here and paid out to them in Germany. Oh yeah! The tears that have been shed in Riga would drown Hitler and the whole Nazi Party over and over and over. The young people are keen and excited at going but the rest are in despair and though many of them damn well deserve their fate it is awful to see the misery in their tear stained faces.

Must wind up as the Censor enclosed a slip in your letter saying that if you wish letters to get there quickly, they must be brief and clearly written — that was one for Lorna I think.

Yours Noons

17

Bulduri
                                        October 16th 1939

My darling Rhona

This is my sixth letter to you — I hope you have had them all. I
go on writing every Sunday. You never saw such a commotion
as was caused by the silly 'Führer's' command to all the Balts,
70,000 in number, to proceed immediately to Germany and
colonize the Polish Corridor. *Everybody* is clearing out, and
there is much weeping and gnashing of teeth — for they have
to leave all their property behind and just take the minimum of
luggage. The Führer is sending forty ships for them and the
voyage will be awful in this cold weather, huddled together in
unheated holds. My poor old blind friend Ada Greditch, aged
eighty-one — is dreading it awfully, but she and all the other
old inmates of the home are obliged to obey. Even the lunatics
from SarkausKalns have to go. Did you ever hear of such a
crazy notion?

What *do* you think? Edith and her mother have gone to
her sister in Bulgaria and have asked us to take charge of their
dog Bellow! He is the dearest and sweetest and best-trained
doggie we have ever had, and we all love him. He follows Una
about like her shadow and sends you his love. God bless you
my darling pet. Don't be homesick, my treasure. I hope you
have got that job and if so do it heartily —

                              Lots of love and kisses

                              Your devoted, loving Granny

                              Lucy Addison (Mumsy)

Bulduri
October 22nd 1939

Sunday

My own darling Rhona

Do not be anxious about us. All is very quiet and peaceful in this dear old place, and for the present we have nothing to fear from the CCCR Bear. We smile at the 'Peaceful Penetration' of the Baltic States; but for the present the Russians are too much taken up with their newly-acquired seaports to bother about the bourgeois. But, as for the evacuation of the wretched Balts, it is the craziest scheme that has ever emanated from the brain of a lunatic. Only the younger generation who worship Hitler are glad to go; but all the others are just heartbroken at being uprooted from the land of their birth, and having to leave everything behind. The anguish I have had to witness beggars description. All our dear old ladies in Mitau are cursing Hitler, and praying that death may overtake them before they have to leave their comfortable 'House for the Aged'. Old Mrs Rosengreen and her room-mate, an old lady of ninety-two, bed-ridden, wring their hands and say 'Hitler is mad'. And the discomfort of the voyage! All huddled together in the cold, without heating or proper sleeping accommodation — you can't think how they dread it. They have been promised all sorts of things when they get to their destination — 42,000 furnished flats etc whereas it stands to reason that nothing but famine and devastation awaits them. In Riga, at present, where it has always been so difficult to find rooms, there are already 10,000 flats being advertised. But enough of this doleful subject. As you say, the Balts did not know when they were well off, and now they will see the difference. I am going tomorrow to take leave of the poor old lady whom you used to take flowers to. She is in despair. Six inmates of the Blind Asylum are included in the list of those who are obliged to go.

God bless you, my very darling child.
Lots of love from your loving old grandmother

Lucy Addison (Mumsy)

19

Tuesday   24th October 1939

Darling Rouite

What a swiz that you didn't get that job — we've been
swanking about it to all your friends — coming from the Consul
one thought it was true. Perhaps something will turn up. At
present everything is quite OK and nobody here is even turning
pink. We shan't even get a smell of the Russian troops for they
are to land at Windau and Libau and keep themselves *to* themselves in the areas allotted to them and will not be allowed to
speak to the population.

The Balt trek is progressing slowly and the whole country
is full of things for sale — houses, estates, millions of pianos
and every conceivable thing. Hellmanns, Freimans, Opolko,
and Mershutz's have had sales down here and they say that the
Flea market is just swamped with articles.

Meantime don't get het up about us — and don't believe
all the alarming rumours you hear or read in the press. This is
the quietest spot in Europe and when the Balts have gone it
will be quite dead. It will be queer to see no familiar faces. As
for the grub — you can buy as much of everything as you
damn well want to — 10 or 100 lbs of butter a day if you like
and all prices are fixed as they were in summer and shops get
strafed if they charge more.

                                                      Noons

Saturday

Bulduri
October 28th 1939

My own darling Rhona

There is no possibility of your coming here in the present unsettled state of things, for if the Bear growls too loud we ourselves might have to evacuate this place, in which case the Legation would have to go too, and the British Minister would see that we Britishers cleared out in time. For the present the Bear is behaving very politely, and gently continues his Peaceful Penetration; but really, darling, don't worry about us, as we are perfectly happy. Keep your pity for the wretched Balts who are being torn from their homes and will have a rude awakening when they get to their destination, if so be they have any illusions and believe in all the marvellous things they have been promised.

I went to town (by train) yesterday, and took leave of some more old friends who are in tears because they have to leave their homes. It is ridiculous to call them the 'Rückwanderer in die Heimat', as most of them have never set foot in the Fatherland in their lives.

God bless you, my beloved child.

Lucy Addison (Mumsy)

Bulduri
November 27th 1939

My darling Rhona

It is such a cruel shame to evacuate all these unhappy Balts. Can you imagine leaving all you possess and going off into such a danger zone? And for a mere bogey. They are still departing at the rate of 2000 a day — there are still about 30,000 idiots to go. There is a persistent rumour that Dr Faust is dead. He was going backwards and forwards in the hospital ships and they say he had a heart stroke. I hope it will have been someone else; he is such a splendid doctor. Some of the Balts, on arriving in Germany, on close inspection of their pedigrees, have been discovered to have a grandfather or great-grandmother of the Jewish persuasion and have been shunted off to a concentration camp. Aren't they brutes? After giving up everything. And the way they are exporting horses and cattle, it is somthink chronic!

> God bless you my darling child
> Your loving grandmother
>
> Lucy Addison (Mumsy)

Don't you dare to acquire a North country accent.

Rhona was by now living in Liverpool.

22

Dorlink Rouite

Yesterday the last of the Balts left and a chapter of history is closed! The *Rundschau* said goodbye with a flourish ' *Wir folgen den Ruf des Führers*' splashed in large print across the front page. Thank God that swinish paper has ceased to exist — it has excelled itself in rudeness and lies about England, getting more and more venomous and if they hadn't closed down and gone I should have gone round and horse-whipped the editor and all his blasted Hunnish Nazi staff. Swines. Every day they printed footling, childish letters supposed to have been written by Balts who were settled in Posen and were quite '*begeistert*' with their reception there — the last letter printed ended 'and don't you believe the reports that there is nothing to eat here and no fuel etc, *das sind alles Englishe Lügen*'! As if anybody in England knows or cares anything about the Balts, whether they go or stay or anything else. Bloody fools. As a matter of fact so many private reports *have* come through that masses have withdrawn at the last minute and on dit that about 15,000 remain here. The *Volksgruppe* itself had to own to 10,000 odd refusing to go and having complained to Hitler that they were treated like dirt here etc they will find it difficult to explain now that all these thousands of badly treated ones prefer to stay and be oppressed by the Letts to going to the Fatherland to enjoy Nazi freedom!

The Rosengreens wrote to Daddy — 'we find it very hard to keep warm in our attic room'! And they were promised a house of their own equal to the houses they gave up here! Most of the Balts are parked out in villages and on farms till room is found for them in Posen — there are still over 200,000 Poles in the town and for these 'barrack' towns are being built in the Warsaw district and as soon as a hut is ready a Polish family is bunged into it and a Balt inherits their lodging in Posen. You can imagine how pleased the ejected Poles are. There are well authenticated reports that many of the incoming Balts have already been murdered, General Hartmann, Brieger (soap

23

factory), Kek and Herrnberger (bakers) amongst others, also rumours of many more having their throats cut by the Poles — there are so many rumours and reports that it is better not to believe any of the tales, but there must be *some* foundation for them because the German wireless announced a couple of days ago that a number of Poles had been executed for murders in Posen. And Erich Hellermann came to say goodbye last week — he is a *Volksgruppe Kreisleiter* and left in a bunch with 1500 of his co-traitors — I asked him what his work in Posen was going to be and he said '*Sicherheit's Kienst*' ie special constable — he said 'we have police and military there but a lot of extra men are needed because the Poles are so revengeful.'

Before they left a lot of these *Kreisleiters* — bumptious young squirts between eighteen to twenty-five yrs of age went to Schwartz's and other restaurants for a final binge — at Schwartz's was a big Jewish looking chap called Peterson and these squirts thinking he was a Jew started baiting him and trying to hustle him out; unfortunately for them Peterson happened to be an ex-champion boxer and he laid six of the Balts out in as many seconds — in the row that followed all Schwartz's fixings got smashed! — another crowd smashed up the Korso and the police arrested dozens of them and fined them 300 Lats each which the German Legation had to pay so as to enable them to get out and catch their ship. A good send off!

The chemists all leaving has created a very difficult situation; thirty-five have gone from Riga and Garber is the only one left in the inner town — there is no chemist in Bolderaa or Dungangriva and forty-five country towns are left without — which means that they have in many cases to send over 100 kilometres to get a prescription made up, as doctors here don't dispense. Kalt the confectioner remains but nearly all the Riga bakers have gone.

Daddy was away nearly a fortnight instead of the two days he expected — he was very lucky to get to Stockholm and back safely for the next boat was captured by the Germans and taken to Stattin where Polish and British passengers were interned — (male ones). He has been away again since his return but only on a night's journey by rail — the sea is no longer safe for such as he for the Huns get information as to who is travelling.

I hope the *Jamakas Sinas** is reaching you OK — our mail is very irregular now that there is no connection with Helsinki any more and we haven't had *The Times* for a fortnight. We think it a great mistake of the Finns not to have come to an agreement with the Bolshis like the other states did — those footling islands were no good to them and it wouldn't have hurt them to give up that small strip near St Petersburg in exchange for the big piece they were offered in the North. The presence of the Bolshis in Libau etc doesn't seem to make any difficulties here and if they keep themselves to themselves as they are now doing it will be OK. Latvia naturally doesn't like it but if they hadn't agreed everything would have gone East by now and so will Finland unless a miracle happens.

Your Little Eva

* a local paper

25

Bulduri
December 18th 1939

Dorlink Rouite

There is nothing on earth for you to worry about on our account — this is the quietest spot in Europe and is going to remain so according to general opinion. The Bolshis are keeping to their agreement and their presence seems to make no difference whatever; naturally it is possible that the country may in time come more under their influence but it will be a matter of getting pale pink and pinker and imperceptibly pinker — by peaceful penetration and *if* so it will be a case of waiting and seeing whether we like it or prefer to return to our native land. The Finnish war cannot affect this country for even if it were (which is unlikely) roped in to help, there would be no fighting here or anywhere near. Nobody has a quarrel with Latvia, it is well-governed and everybody is happy — it is a quiet backwater now that those Balts have cleared and one is no longer afraid of Nazi interference — and it is a land of plenty. Therefore there is no reason to think that anything will change suddenly.

The journey now costs about £50 as communication is difficult now but in spring there will be plenty of air services. And I had better tell you what Daddy said when I told him you had got the job after all. He said 'Thank goodness — I wonder if she knows how lucky she is.' I said 'Yes I think she is pleased to have something to do' and he said 'She must realize that the days when young people of her age stay at home and loaf are over now — there will be no more horse-keeping or allowance.' Daddy thinks that if the horizon does get pink the factory may get nationalized and mebbe the houses too — in which case we should all have to go and live in Karia's butka as three rooms is the very most one would be allowed!! Poor Daddy it would be very hard on him after the struggle he has had to get things going.

Yours Noons

Dorlink Rouite

We have the coldest spell Latvia ever remembers having −42° of frost at Gaizinkala −38° in Riga and here — Celsino −28½° Réamur, that is 70° of frost Fahrenheit. Every damn pipe in our house is frozen up — The smith worked here all day yesterday melting us out and two hours after he'd gone we were frozen up again. I heat the stoves twice a day and all the fires are roaring yet the house is icy — only the growlery is habitable. I am out all day chopping and carting and keep as warm as anything with three sweaters and five pairs of pants on! Poor Pinchka and minch* are huddled in their caboose, come out to feed and scuttle back like mad. Bellow walks on three legs — holding up each in turn but soon warms up when he sees a crow to chase. The streets are empty — nobody goes out unless they must. Everybody's waterworks and central heating are bust and all the bottles in all the shops have burst — beer, lemonade, seltzers etc, all potatoes and vegs frozen too. We had two days blizzard before the frost and the snow is just perfect for skiing when it gets warmer.

Your own Noons

* the cat and kittens

My own darling Rhona

There is snow everywhere. We had another snowfall last night,
at least six inches Uni says, and she was up early sweeping and
ploughing. Of course she loves it, and she is the only one of us
who is not petrified with cold, for she wears several pairs of
socks, four pairs of pants and four jerseys and blouses. She
works much too hard. I don't know what we should do without her — and, as you say, she certainly is awfully generous.
She gives everything away and keeps nothing for herself. Ganf
gave her a ticket for a Beethoven Symphony Concert at the
Opera House one Friday, conducted by Leo Blech. It was
superb and the house packed. We enjoyed listening to it on the
wireless.

The Russians have commandeered the Lettish ice-breaker
but I doubt whether any earthly ice-breaker will succeed in
opening the Libau harbour. The Baltic is frozen stiff and also
our Bay.

God bless you, my Treasure.
Love and kisses from your devoted, loving grandmother

Lucy Addison

Bulduri
January 22nd 1940

Dorlink Rouite

I went to a Beethoven Concert at the Opera last week, Leo Blech conducting — what mutts the Nazi's are to scrap a man like that and the idiotic part of it is that they still play records of him conducting the Berlin Philharmonic from Dutschland-sender. Silly asses. The opera was *packed* and so many people couldn't get tickets that they are repeating the concert next week.

Yours Noons

Dorlink Rouite

There's not much to write about 'cept snow and ice, blizzards and frost — the most glorious winter since I was a kid, there are such masses of snow that one walks between walls of it and poor Bellow gets very bored because he can't see over the top and can only hear what is going on on the other side of the street! He seems to love it though and gets sudden spasms of bounding into the deep snow head down and burrowing round in circles at top speed, all you see is his tail end and a cloud of snow and he comes out caked so that he can't see out of his eyes. So far the blizzards have come so soon after each other that my shovelling hasn't been able to keep pace and there has been no time left for skiing.

Your own Noons

Dorlink Rouite

It is colder than ever here —24° Réamur again this morning and
a cutting wind; there is a terrible shortage of fuel and all the
spare men from town are working in the forests and anyone
having a horse has to help carting out the timber. The amount
of people who have got frostbitten is terrible — mostly drunks
— farm people driving home from market after a drop too
much, fall asleep and arrive home with dead hands and feet
and have to have them amputated. Several cases of people
tight — falling out of their sledges and freezing to death too. A
farmer had been missing for ten days horse and sledge and all
and yesterday a forester found the whole caboodle in the forest
— the man was frozen dead on the sledge and the horse had
wandered into the forest, got itself so tied up in the reins that it
couldn't move and had just stood there all that time — it was
just skin and bone and so weak from starvation and cold that it
could scarcely stand.

Yours ever Noony

*The 30th April 1940 was the Addisons' 57th wedding anniver-
sary. The weather had remained bitterly cold and they heard
enviously the news of Rhona's move to Bermuda. But by then the
post was no longer getting through. Because she could not write to
her granddaughters, Lucy Addison began, in September 1942, on
Ganf's 83rd birthday, to write an account of the war years. She
kept it up until the end of 1944 when the Nazis retreated and the
Addisons returned to Bulduri — and when she could again write
her weekly letters.*

31

PART

2

I must begin to try and tell you of all the vicissitudes we have passed through since the outbreak of this disastrous war that has separated us from you so completely. I know you must have been very worried about us, my darling, when you heard first about the Bolsheviks and then the Germans coming to these wretched Baltic provinces.

Well, here goes!

The last time we heard from you was just on the eve of England's declaration of war; when Quen very rightly said: surely they are not going to war because of Danzig and the Polish Corridor. Little did our statesmen foresee the disastrous consequences of such a step; yet, had they let Hitler take Poland with impunity, he would not have stopped there, and there was bound to be war anyhow.

In the meantime the amazing so-called 'repatriation' of the Balts started. Never was such an exodus since the days of Moses and Pharoah! '*Hitler ruft!*' was their slogan and at his bidding these foolish, deluded people left their houses, their estates, their farms, their business, shops, everything. The local paper, *Rundschau,* grew daily more hysterical, threatening those who remained behind with untold tortures and Bartholomew nights at the hands of the Letts. Scores of steamers, even ocean liners were sent to Riga from the Fatherland to convey them all to the *Heimat* [Homeland] which very few of them had ever seen or cared tuppence about. All the nobility left first; then the land proprietors; the farmers with their cattle; the clergy; 700 doctors; chemists; bankers; men of business; shopkeepers; factory owners; old men and women from the almshouses; prisoners; convicts; inmates of lunatic asylums; the sick from the hospitals; even two or three blind girls from the Blind Asylum. Before leaving they bought up all the boots and shoes, underwear, suits, frocks and winter coats in the town. All our Baltic friends came to bid us goodbye, heartbroken at leaving their old homes, very uncertain as to the future awaiting them, yet unable to disregard the call of the Fuhrer. Each of them was promised a replica of their homes here:

35

landed proprietors were to have their estates, farmers their farms; chemists their apothecary shops, hairdressers their *Friseur* establishments. One old maid said to me: 'I àm to have a flat of four rooms, a balcony and a kitchen, just like the one I have here.' The Rosengreens paid us a farewell visit, and Karin said: 'Hitler says Britain will cease to exist. It will vanish off the map of Europe. There will be nothing left of England but a little heap of ashes.' We shall see!

The *Rundschau* waxed daily ruder and more abusive towards England, and finally the Editor and all his staff plus the printing-press left to set up another scavenger paper in the Warthegau, the part of Poland where most of the Balts settled down; but not before I had written him a letter, telling him just what I thought of him and his *Dreck* [filthy] paper, signing myself *'Ein langjahriger Abonnent der RR.'* [A longtime subscriber].

The town seemed very empty after they had all gone, and all the old shops, like Scheuber, Mentzendorff, Gorke, the chemists and hundreds of others, as well as all the confectioners cafés and restaurants were closed. Only the Jewish shops, like Feiterlberg, Thal and Arenstamm remained.

To return to more personal matters.

The winter of 1939-1940 was the severest we have ever known. From the middle of December till the beginning of April we scarcely had one day without hard frost. Ganf's weather report for three and a half months is all flaming red. Day after day and night after night we have temperatures of −20° to −30° Réamur, with the result that our beautiful beeches, the Pyramid Oak, Ganf's beloved rhododendrons, many chestnut trees and our famous apple trees were all killed. Whereas those three apple trees had had only two apples between them in 1938, they bore 3000 in 1939. Ten million apple trees perished in Latvia, so that we had no fruit at all all the winter.

All that winter darling Ganf was very ill. Unable to shave he grew a white beard (which I sent you) and he looked very handsome with it. Mrs Orde who frequently visited him, used to call him 'Moses'. When the summer came, however, he was able to toddle about the garden, and bask in the sun on the verandah of the summerhouse. On 21st June, being the longest day, Uni ordered a taxi and we drove down to the beach, hired some chairs and sat and watched the sunset. That was a red-letter day, for we had neither of us seen the sea for munce and munce [months and months]. As that expedition did him no harm, Uni persuaded us to go to the Lido twice to see the 'Scotties', a company of Scotch lads and lassies in Highland dress with a bandmaster aged fourteen who was a perfect marvel. They played on various instruments; they sang Scotch songs and danced, led with astonishing vim by the little boy in a kilt and an Eton jacket.

In the meantime in the beginning of June the peaceful penetration of these provinces by the Bolos [Bolsheviks] was going forward steadily. They established their naval base at Libau and Windau and gradually sent their armies to Riga. When the first contingent of the latter arrived, they were met by enthusiastic mobs of Jews and Communists from the Moscow suburbs, waving red flags, and there was some street fighting, bloodshed and great excitement. At first the Russians had orders to keep themselves to themselves, and not to interfere in any way with the aborigines. If you asked a Russian officer any questions, his invariable answer was: 'Read the papers.' Never having seen so much food in their lives they bought up all the hams, sausages, meat, fowls and cereals they could lay hands on; and all the cafés and restaurants teemed with Russians devouring cakes and sweets and drinking chocolate with whipped cream. They had a glorious time!

Besides that they bought up all the boots and shoes; haberdashery; fountain pens, gold and silver watches and jewellery. Their wives and children, all in rags and tatters arrived in Riga in trainloads, and were soon fitted out in elegant garments, their hair dressed in the latest style, and manicured and all. Then, having established themselves firmly, they started nationalizing houses, factories, banks, shops and business firms. Our factory was seized and so were our two houses. They sent men to measure the outsides of the houses, and other men to measure the rooms inside, the idea being that each individual is only allowed nine square feet. They professed astonishment at the number of our bedrooms. 'What do you want with a separate bedroom for each person?' they said. 'We sleep seven or eight in one room.' 'Very unhygienic,' says I.

Gradually the schools were reformed. The schoolmasters were turned out and Communists put in their places. Religion was abolished and all the books confiscated, and the wretched children had to be taught without books, just on little scraps of paper. They were taught to worship Stalin as their god. This style of thing: 'Children, pray to your God to send you some chocolate.' The children prayed. Nothing happened. 'Now pray to Father Stalin!' and chocolates for each child materialized.

The booksellers and lending libraries were ransacked by gangs of women and all Bibles, hymn-books and religious works, besides anti-Communist literature and novels concerning Kings and Queens or highlife, were burned. Fairy tales and children's stories shared the same fate, for children were not to be taught a pack of lies about fairies and goblins and that sort of twaddle. From their earliest years they must learn practical things and their picture books should contain nothing but aeroplanes, submarines, guns and other useful things.

Towards autumn things became so weird that Sir Stafford Cripps, the British Ambassador in Moscow advised all Britishers in Latvia to leave the country. Gradually the Legation, the Consulate and Passport Office were liquidated. The Chaplain left, and so did the Minister, the Consul and all their staffs. I was very sorry to say goodbye to Mrs Orde, who had been exceedingly kind to us, and who had supplied us with biscuits, fruit and other delicacies (unobtainable in Riga) all during Ganf's illness; and before leaving brought us an immense box of groceries, soap, clothes, etc, some of which we could use ourselves and the rest we distributed among our friends. Mr Orde had been appointed British Minister to Chile, and his wife was going to England to see her boys before joining him. Mr Orde took seventy-two days to reach his destination, via Siberia and Japan ... meeting his wife at Panama. The Bentons, Hobsons and Dorriecorrie went to England via Siberia and the USA, Paul Frawcke to Sofia. Mr Trant [the Consul] urged us to leave this country too, and we obtained leave from both the FO in England and Sweden to go to Stockholm; but after all we decided to stay put here, and we have never regretted it.

Then all the British colony left Riga in a special train to Vladivostok and thence to Australia via Japan; and touching at Shanghai (or was it Hong Kong) where they sent an SOS for summer garments, having nothing but fur coats and warm things. Of course, lots of clothes were sent in answer to their appeal. The whole journey and voyage were at the expense of the British government. Only Mrs Eckert insisted on remaining behind, saying that she had a weak heart and wanted to be buried beside her husband; and sure enough a month or six weeks after her sister had left, she succumbed to a heart attack (angina pectoris) and died at the hospital at the age of seventy. I never dreamt she was as old as that. We miss her Wednesday visits; she was such a sport! Gladys, Miss Pain and Miss Cathcart who all loathe each other were made to share a compartment in the train, and a cabin on board the ship to Australia. I guess there were wigs on the green by the time they got there.

Dick and Madgie had hired a sweet little bungalow on the bank of Aa and spent some very pleasant summer months there. We visited them several times and dined with them once. But in the early autumn they went back to town. They said life in the country was becoming more and more of a nightmare, and so they decided to follow the example of the rest of the Britishers and quit. So they started selling their things till the Russians came and laid embargo on them ... and, after bidding us a sad farewell, they travelled to Vancouver Island via Siberia and Japan and eventually landed in England.

In the meantime Dad's mill being in the hands of the Bolshis, and he practically turned out, Mailand, the blacksmith, or rather locksmith, was elected Director in his place; the whole office staff was dismissed, and workmen put into the places of cashier, bookkeeper etc presided over by ignorant Russian Commissars who created as much confusion as possible. Dad, however, insisted on going up to the mill every day and working in any capacity, so as to keep in touch with his beloved factory. The hands were made to work at top speed for ten hours a day, and to attend lectures in the evening, all of which they hated. They were to be educated! You can imagine the wrath of the elly double tees [Letts]. Huge pictures of Lenin and Stalin decorated all the walls, besides daily news bulletins and placards in every department (part of the education), also denounciations by the hands of their fellow-workmen, such as 'Emily Birch goes to the lav too often and stays there too long.' Result: E.B. gets strafed.

Now it was decreed that the Director Mailand and his family should have Dad's house at the seaside, he and Lina being permitted to live in the dining room and to use the kitchen and bathroom. This must have been gall and wormwood to poor Dad. The garden too, was taken away from him. Lina's old mother, her aunt and Minna had been living in Dad's house for about a year. Now they had to evacuate it and he hired a villa for the three old ladies and paid the rent for two years in advance. Dad was contemplating going to Finland, and so he started selling his furniture, books etc. At the same time people were being arrested daily and nightly and carried off in a Black Maria (only she happened to be green) to unknown destinations by the Cheka. It was a ghastly time and nobody felt safe.

That winter was bitterly cold too, almost more severe than the last, and Dad's fine orchard was completely destroyed. Towards the end of November 1940 Ully Baby [Ganf] fell ill again. We have a very good doctor, Liesniek, who seemed to understand his rather mysterious case and always gave him relief with injections and various medicines. It was a very anxious time for Noony and me. We had a nurse for him, but he would not have anything to do with her. We kept her a month and then let her go. She said she had never had such a perfect rest and holiday in her life. By Christmas we were able to move Ganf into my bedroom for the day, it being more sunny than his. We had a tiny Xmas tree in a flowerpot; but it was rather sad. We missed all our darlings, and not even Daddy came to it. Ganf does not remember a thing about the winter.

He, who never expressed a wish for anything to eat, said

one day: 'I should so like to have some preserved apricots or peaches!' So Uni ransacked the town for tinned fruit — but in vain. It had all been sold out. Then I wrote to Ina Shalit and asked her if her mother could spare me one or two tins — and the very next day the dear child arrived with Hirschberg, and brought us two tins of delicious fruit, which kept Ganf going for a long time. Hirschberg said he would try to get us some more. Ina told us her father had died; her mother was obliged to go out and work (like everybody else) and she herself was studying at the University. She looked very sweet in a red frock. Little did I think I should never see her again!

Sure enough, after some weeks Hirschberg turned up with another tin of preserved fruit. He had supper with us, and we gave him some English books. About a fortnight later Hurevitz, another Hebrew, turned up with two more tins of preserved fruit. He said he had heard from Hirschberg that Ganf was ill and had a fancy for fruit. They all refused payment, and Hurevitz said there was nothing in the world he wouldn't do for Ganf.

When Hitler made his first great speech, which lasted a whole hour, Ganf came down to listen to it, and after that he came down every day and sat before the fire till bedtime, enjoying the wireless and having his meals with us.

In April the Bolshis came, looked over the house and ordered us to clear out by May. We started hurriedly selling our furniture, pictures, clothes, hundreds of books etc with a view to collecting money for our flight to Sweden par avion, for we were allowed only a minimum of luggage. Not being used to selling, we gave everything away far too cheap. Still the money kept us going for a whole year. We also gave heaps of things away to all our old neighbours and friends, for we were determined not to leave a stick of furniture for the Bs.

One afternoon Mrs Irbe brought a Swedish gentleman to us, to ask if we could let him have a room, as he could not find a suitable one anywhere. We said we could not oblige him, as we were dismantling the house preparatory to leaving it. Uni volunteered to find him a room, and so we offered him a cup of coffee, and he sat and talked to Ganf for more than an hour in the most beautiful German, and his conversation was so interesting that Ganf asked him to drop in again for a chat, after which he often looked in and we invited him to tea now and then and liked him very much. He was of strikingly aristocratic appearance, about seven feet in height, beautifully groomed, and so like the King of Sweden though much younger and not so ugly, that we always called him the 'King of Sweden'. You can imagine his astonishment once when they were having a heated argument, Ganf said: '*Aber mein lieber König von Schweden* ... !' I then told him that we had christened him thus, after which he gave us his card. More of him and his tragic fate anon.

After all we decided not to go to Sweden but to stay quietly here. Cariah* offered to take us in and we accepted her offer. So we sent the needful furniture to her house and at last the sad day, Sunday the 4th of May arrived, and we left the dear old home where we had lived so happily for fifty years, and flitted to Cariah's, where we settled down very easily. Poor darling Uni, who had worked like a horse at packing and carting wheelbarrow-loads of things across, fell ill. She would go on toiling, but at last she gave in. With a temperature of over 40° she lay on that draughty verandah. She stayed on in that empty house (with Bellow) for a few days after we left, and in the daytime sat in a solitary armchair in front of the fire in the large empty drawing room. She felt very weak for some time after — no strength in her legs. Alide came down and helped us, and for the rest of the summer she came once a week to give Noony a day off.

Uni had moved the children's summerhouse from our garden to Cariah's on a huge lorry, and turned it back to front, taking down the back wall, so that it was open, facing the street. We arranged it as a room for me to give my lessons in and fitted up with a carpet, curtains, a sofa, chairs and a table, bookshelves, pictures and a hanging lamp it was most attractive, and the envy and admiration of all comers. There were some wicker chairs and a table under a tree close by for outdoor lessons in fine weather. The little balcony on the reverse side served as a bedroom for Noony. I appropriated a room in

* friend of the family

Cariah's shed and turned it into an elegant dressing room and had my morning tub al fresco in the lilac bushes. We all three enjoyed those summer months. Ganf used to go down to the sea most mornings, and to the river in the afternoon; and very often he went to the old garden and sat on the steps of the tennis-house and dreamt of the *tempi passati* and all the wonderful times we had in that dear place.

Now all the inhabitants of the Baltic provinces had to become Russian subjects and to petition for Russian passports. We were exempt from this 'privilege' but had to have a 'permit' to reside here, to be renewed every four months. At a meeting at Majori the Commissar asked the crowd: 'What sort of people are the Addisons?' Chorus of voices: 'Oh they are very popular; very kind to the poor, the sick and the blind etc ... ' 'Yes, so I have heard before,' said the Commissar. Then he went on to ask about the Irbes and others. For some reason Dad was only given a permit for four days at a time, which had to be constantly renewed.

About this time came a ghastly period of arrests of men and women, and kidnapping of children. In all 45,000 Letts were seized, examined, often tortured and finally transported to Siberia or other remote parts of Russia. Many people we knew were thus carried off; eg the oculist Dr Emerson, his wife and two sons. Mrs Emerson and her youngest son were pupils of mine. They have a lovely villa and garden in the woods. One day a lorry, packed with weeping and lamenting folk, stopped at their gate; two men rushed in and said: 'You've got to come with us. Hurry up!' Mrs Emerson fainted. They said: 'That's the best way. No protestations, no fuss!' They picked her up, flung her into the lorry, took the youngest son (my pupil), aged fourteen, and went off. Of course the moment they were out of sight their house was pillaged. The doctor and his eldest son were collected in town. They had not been given time to take even a toothbrush with them.

Mrs Sparnin recently (1945) had a letter from the eldest son from Yeniseiski in Siberia. *Mirabele dictu* the family had not been separated. They were living together. The doctor was working at the hospital; Mrs Emerson was doing the housekeeping. Freddy was working on the railway, and Yuri was

43

studying at the technical school. They kept pigs, and were doing fairly well, though frightfully homesick.

Another of my pupils, Elsie Cooper, aged twelve, was out when the *Bourreaux* came to their house and carried off her mother. When she got back the poor child 'she sobbed and she sighed and she bitterly cried' and she started off to town in search of her mother; they were neither of them heard of again. The third case was the father of my pupil Aina Burke. He was a Lettish officer who was taken to Siberia and has vanished completely. There was wailing and gnashing of teeth and panic everywhere, no one knowing who was to be the next victim. The worst of it was that in most cases the families were separated: the men being sent in one direction, their wives in another, and the unfortunate children by themselves. The cruelty of it!

In the meantime Hitler had invaded Russia on a front (as he boasted) reaching from the White Sea in the North to the Black Sea in the South. Having taken Lithuania and Esthonia he was now marching towards Riga with his famous *Wehrmacht*. The German Navy was approaching Libau and Windau, and the Red Army and Navy were in full flight. Streams and streams of soldiers and sailors were passing down our street towards the river, grimy, weary and footsore. They said their officers had all got away by sea and ordered them to march to Berlin. They had no ordnance maps and were completely ignorant of geography. Some of the NCO's asked Uni to direct them to Berlin. She drew a diagram in the sand and showed then how to get to Riga first. Whey they got across the Aa over the floating bridge those weary soldiers, with blistered and bleeding feet, cast off their boots, their knapsacks and other impedimenta and continued their route barefoot. Lots of people went across the river and collected those things; and Noony brought home a knapsack, some drinking mugs and other odds and ends.

After them came an endless procession of Hebrews, who had had orders to quit the seaside at a moment's notice. It was pathetic to see them toiling along, many of them carrying their children on their backs. I spoke to one old lady who seemed in great distress. She was too exhausted to keep up with her family and had been left behind. She had hastily packed all her valuables in the suitcase, but not having the strength to carry it, had abandoned it on the road. She said she had no stick or umbrella to walk with, so I gave her a walking-stick and bade her god-speed. We heard afterwards that many of these unfortunates, soldiers, sailors and Jews had perished on the road to Riga, being bombed by German aeroplanes.

On June 22nd 1941 we had our first air raid, which was a very interesting sight. On the following day I was sitting in the garden, giving a lesson to a youth of nineteen whom I call 'Boy Blue', when suddenly there was a terrific explosion, which made me jump sky-high, while he fell off his chair flat on his face. The Russians had blown up the railway bridge — prematurely, so that they were unable to get their tanks and lorries etc across the river. So there they stuck, rows and rows of them, as well as many trainloads of ammunition, reaching from Edinburg station to the railway bridge.

They accordingly resolved to blow up the ammunition trains, and everyone living within a mile or more of the railway lines was warned to evacuate their houses and seek shelter in the woods. We made up bundles of clothes etc and went to bed without undressing, but nothing happened. Ganf slept in his clothes for three nights and still nothing happened. It was pathetic to see a string of men, women and children, babies in prams, cats and dogs, trekking every evening in fair weather and foul, to spend the night in the woods. Our house being empty became a refuge for all the people living on the river bank in the vicinity of the bridges. Every room was occupied; Schinderkungs with his wife and seven children lived in the growlery. Ugh! At length it was decided to dump the ammunition into the river, after which those wretched people presumably slept comparatively peacefully in their beds. In the meantime it had transpired that trainloads of the so-called ammunition contained the result of wholesale looting of the contents of the shops in Libau and Windau and other towns, and so the inhabitants of Bulduri vied with each other in pinching materials, and thoroughly enjoyed themselves. At a later date, however, having denounced each other, they were compelled by the Huns to give up their ill-gotten goods.

All the time the foe was steadily advancing on Riga from three different directions. On June 23rd Riga was bombarded by the Huns and a great deal of damage was done. Whole streets were wiped out; St Peter's Church, the Town Hall and Schwarzhaupterhaus were destroyed, and our English Church, built by my grandfather, was badly damaged, all the beautiful stained glass windows, save one, broken. Fierce air raids and street fights took place. The bridges were stormed. The Bavarian regiment, (according to the King of Sweden, who visited their general, an old friend of his, in hospital) lost a hundred men while crossing the railway bridge which was subsequently blown up by the Russians, as were all the other bridges. Several thousand Russian soldiers being quartered at the Ilgeciern mill, the factory came in for some rough treatment. All the windows were smashed and five people were killed, amongst them was the old gatekeeper's wife, the gardener's daughter and a girl in the office.

On Sunday June 29th Riga was taken; and on July 1st the Germans marched into Bulduri, and were received with great enthusiasm by the Letts whom they had delivered from their tormentors. They were very cocky and boasted that it would not be many days before Petersburg fell. Fortunately we had laid in a few stores, for the Huns soon ransacked all the shops and left them empty. They did not molest us, and we went on living quite peacefully for some time. I always slept with my window open. One morning at 3 am I heard someone rattling at the gate. I got out of bed, and saw two young soldiers trying to get in. I went out and opened the gate and they begged leave to come in and have a wash. They said they were pioneers and had cycled all night and were very dusty. Uni and I provided them with water, soap and towels; then we gave them some sandwiches and a bottle of beer, for all of which they were very grateful. They called out to a comrade who was looking after their bicycles: '*Hör mal Schmidt, hier sind Engländer! Sie haben uns eine Flasche Bier gegeben.*' One of them was very anxious about his mother, who he said lived at Essen, which was constantly being bombarded by the RAF.

On July 21st I went to see Lina's mother and aunt who lived close to the Synagogue at the back of Cariah's. Whilst talking to them I noticed that the old caretaker of the Synagogue, the Jewish cobbler Michelson was staggering under the weight of the windows which were being taken out; the massive doors, as well as the pews and benches were also being removed. I went round to enquire the reason for this proceeding and was told that the Commandant had given orders that the Synagogue should be blown up at 8 pm. The three old ladies were very much alarmed; so I went and told Dad who promised to look after them. Then I went home and insisted on all the windows being opened because there was to be an explosion at eight. Ganf refused to believe it, and Cariah pooh-poohed the idea, and when, at exactly eight o'clock there were five distinct detonations, she said: 'So much for your great explosion!' But immediately afterwards came an almighty explosion, and the whole building crashed down and burst into flames. We afterwards learnt that the poor old caretaker, his wife, son and daughter, as well as the stranger within his gates had been lined up inside of the Synagogue and shot. Hence the five detonations. I mingled with the crowd that stood watching the conflagration with great glee, and I was so furious I could not help telling them that I thought it was wicked, horrible, devilish; and that whether it was a Lutheran Church, or Orthodox, or a Jewish Synagogue, it was *God's house*, a house of prayer, and no one had a right to destroy it. Those whom I addressed in my wrath, melted away, for fear of being seen listening to such anti-German heresy. Dad and Lina spent the night on the roof of the old ladies' cottage, pouring buckets of water over it. The Synagogue burnt fiercely all night, and the heat and the glare were intense.

We were horrified one day to see notices posted up everywhere, saying that all Britishers, Russians and Hebrews were to evacuate the seaside within twenty-four hours. We immediately went to the Commandant, who lived at the Casino, and petitioned to be allowed to stay, pleading our age and the fact that we had lived there for fifty years and had never meddled with politics. He was quite a decent fellow and seemed inclined to grant our request; but he was obliged to ask leave of the Commandant West (West being Hagensberg). Uni listened to him arguing over the phone for a quarter of an hour. Among other things he said: 'They are both quite harmless, both past eighty. Think of it! Eighty and eighty are 160!' But the other old beast said: 'An Englishman is dangerous, even at ninety.' So it was settled that we should retire to within ten kilometres of the war-zone. We then asked for and obtained five days' grace, in order to look out for a suitable abode. Dad and Lina had already cleared out of Bulduri some time before. They packed the remains of their furniture etc on a lorry, and perched on the top of their luggage they drove off to Ilgeciem. When Dad heard of our plight he at once asked us to join him and live in the Halls' house at the factory. Accordingly we flitted thither on August 26th 1941. Mr Sparnin lent us two lorries for our furniture. We hired a horse and carriage for Ganf and me, and taking a mournful leave of Cariah and all the neighbours who had come to see us off, we drove to Ilgeciem in very fine weather, Uni following on her bike, and the faithful Bellow running behind. Lina had laid the table and prepared a nice supper for us, with lots of flowers. Dad gave us five rooms: a dining room, a large drawing room and two bedrooms upstairs and a small bedroom for Uni downstairs. He was awfully kind to us, only he objected to Bellow, so we asked Alide to take charge of him, and he had a very happy home there. Alide had come to help us arrange the rooms, and were soon shipshape and very comfortably installed. Daddy had two rooms on the same floor, and constantly dropped in for a chat.

One day Herr Senff, who belonged to the firm of H & A Gratenau in Bremen, brought us greetings and a present of money from Ganf's agents. He had just lost his wife and he brought his son Wolfgang, a charming boy of fourteen — and bewailed the fact that there was no German school in Riga to send him to. So I offered to teach him English. He gladly accepted and asked if I could teach him Swedish as well; and so he came five times a week for both languages, and made astounding progress. I never wish for a keener or more intelligent pupil. Strange to say, though Ilgeciem is so out of the way, I always had lots of pupils. Some of them came all the way from Bulduri twice a week, and others from town. If I lived on the moon, I should get pupils! I had as many as eighteen at Ilgeciem.

48

Our life at Ilgeciem was serene and placid. Ganf and I used to go to the Kuckucksberg, five minutes' walk from the mill, for our daily constitutional. The Kuckucksberg had originally been a range of sandhills, and had been converted into a lovely park by a clever landscape gardener. There were seats everywhere, and an amphitheatre for outdoor performances. There was a fine view over the town and the river from the topmost hill. When it was too hot to climb hills we used to go through our garden to a field belonging to the factory, and lie down in the sun. We often had visitors such as the Smalls, and Ellises, Mr Lawson and stray Balts from the Fatherland. Occasionally we went to the Kaiserwald to have tea with the Smalls, and once we went to a cinema and saw a German film, which was not very edifying.

The Opera house was reserved for the Wehrmacht, but once Noony was given a ticket for *The Flying Dutchman* and thoroughly enjoyed it. Cariah came most Sundays — often on foot, because there were no trains. Such was the extent of our dissipations.

The food question was rather a problem. Our rations were quite insufficient. We had the same ration-cards as the Letts, whereas the *Reichsdeutsche* hogs got *twice* the amount of food on theirs, and the unfortunate Jews *half* what we had. Uni was indefatigable in catering for us, and thanks to her we never really felt the pangs of hunger. Uni sold her wellingtons for a small joint of pork and a kilo of lard; her evening dress and shoes for oatmeal, manna and other cereals. I parted with towels and other things for sugar, and we occasionally sold Ganf's shirts or pants. The Russian money we still had was no good, as the Huns had introduced Marks and Pfennigs.

Thanks to the generosity of our humble friends at Bulduri we were better off than most people. One old market woman insisted on sending us a fowl or duck now and then, saying: 'You can pay me when the war is over, and if I die before that, all the better for you.' Others sent us eggs, bacon and other delicacies; Mrs Sparnin sent us milk, tomatoes, butter and home-made bread every Saturday. Mrs Juniper presented us with grapes and melons, and one fisherman's wife twice sent us ten Marks, which we did not like to refuse for fear of hurting

49

her feelings. It was all very touching. Noony used to go miles on her bike to fetch milk. In fact, considering the times, we lived in the lap of luxury, and were able to share our food with many less fortunate friends. Besides that Mr Krommer used to keep Ganf in cigars, cigarettes and pipe tobacco. In addition to that, he once presented us with a ham — an unheard-of luxury.

Trevy, Lina, Uni — in fact all British subjects were obliged to go to Riga twice a week to report themselves at the *'Sicherheitspolizei'* [Security Police]. I wrote a petition asking for us old folks to be exempt from this formality by reason of our age and infirmities, and though, with their usual courtesy they did not vouchsafe a reply, yet they left us in peace and did not molest us at all. Uni was most conscientious and never went to Bulduri, but made appointments with Mrs Sparnin, Lina's aunt and Minna and others to meet her on the other side of the Aa and bring her milk and sundry other commodities not available elsewhere. She used often to meet a little old lady, who always gave her a friendly nod, and one day Noony stopped to speak to her. The Old Dear (as we always call her now) asked Noony if her mother's maiden name was Hill; and the reply being in the affirmative, she said that sixty-eight years ago, when she was twelve and I eighteen, I had offered to teach her German. She was the daughter of our concierge; and she said that owing to those wonderful (?) lessons she had been able to get into the German *Töchterschule* where she received such a good education that she got a situation as governess to a well-known patrician family in Riga with whom she lived forty-three years and educated three generations of children. She travelled with the family to Vienna, Nice, Monte Carlo and other fashionable resorts, and at one time spent two years in Germany; and just before the German Exodus in 1940 she bought a lovely cottage with a huge garden on the Schlochsche Strasse beyond Nordeckshof with her savings and she took her widowed sister, Mrs Tilting, and her family to live with her. She declared that she owed her successful career to my lessons. Uni then asked her to come and see us at Ilgeciem. On the appointed day she arrived with an enormous bouquet of flowers. I folded her in my arms and said: *'Ach, meine kleine Schülerin!'* though I must confess I had not the faintest recollection of those German lessons. She said that she was passing a garden full of showy flowers; she went in and asked the owner if she would sell her some. The woman said: 'Certainly. Do you want them for a wedding, or a funeral, or what?!' The Old Dear replied: 'They are for an English lady.' 'What is her name?' 'Addison.' 'Oh,' exclaimed the woman, 'take every flower in my garden free, gratis and for nothing, for many years ago, when I and my sister were orphans, living with a cruel aunt at the railway-crossing at Edinburg, the Addison children used to come every Christmas Eve in their sledges with their little ponies and bring us Christmas trees laden with sweets and gingerbreads, besides toys and clothes!' Subsequently this woman, Natalie Fälit, often came to see us at Ilgeciem and brought us flowers, potatoes and other vegetables from her garden. A third coincidence occurred once when Noony was on her way to Pinkenhof in search of milk and her bike came to grief and she went into a farmhouse and begged leave to dump her bike there till she returned. The farmer's wife said 'Aren't you Miss Addison?' and then came the same story of the Christmas trees and gingerbreads, and it turned out that she was Natalie's sister Dorit. Ever since then she has supplied us with milk, delicious home-made bread, and eggs; and whenever she killed a pig or a calf she sent us some veal, pork or brawn. You must know that nobody saw a drop of milk from year's end to year's end — and as for meat, we only got $^1/_2$d worth of cat's meat once a week — so we were marvellously privileged, and able to share the good things with our friends. Another blessing was that we were able to get soup every day (except Sunday) from the workmen's soup kitchen at the factory. This was a great help to Noony who did the cooking. Dad took it too.

One day Ganf was reading, when suddenly he exclaimed: 'My right eye has gone phutt!' And sure enough, he had suddenly gone blind on that eye. He went to an oculist once or twice, but alas! there was nothing to be done. It is tragic, especially as he is so fond of reading. He can scarcely read at all now; but he is wonderfully patient and uncomplaining. I read aloud to him three times a day. Thank goodness he can see to find his way about, and to play patience, which is his only distraction, poor darling!

I wrote several petitions for us to be allowed to go back to the Strand, if only for a few months in summer; but no notice was taken of them. At the beginning of October 1942 a young Esthonian officer from the '*Sicherheitspolizei*' came to me and asked for English lessons. I gladly took him on. During the first lesson I asked if he could not put in a word for us at the SP and obtain leave for us to go down to the seaside now and again. 'Why ask leave?' said he, 'Just you go down and enjoy yourselves, and no one will be any the wiser.' Emboldened by his advice, Ganf and I set off for Bulduri the very next day. Cariah was out when we got there, and when she came home and saw us sitting on her verandah steps with our suitcases, she nearly had a fit. We spent a couple of very pleasant days there. Ganf took his favourite walks, and I visited Mrs Sparnin and all my old friends. Uni came to fetch us and pilot us home, for getting in and out of the overcrowded trains and trams is positively dangerous for old people. Dad was immensely tickled at our escapade and lost no time in following our example, and he and Lina thoroughly enjoyed walking along the beach and seeing all the familiar places. On 6th November we went down again and stayed with Cariah for a few days. One day at dinner Ganf gave us an awful shock by slipping off his chair on to the floor in a faint. I jumped up, caught my foot in the carpet and came down flat on my face. And there we lay, heads and tails, till I was able to scramble up on to my feet. We helped Ganf up and led him to an armchair by the fire and to my surprise he said: 'Give me my cigarette, it is on the piano.' He was all right again and had no recollection of having fainted. Twice since then he has had similar attacks.

About that time Isa Krommer and her little boy Sven came from their home in Corinthia to spend a couple of months with her husband. They came several times to spend the day with us, and we loved their visits.

Noony's long-suffering Sunbeam [bicycle] gradually went to pieces on the rough roads, and she was reduced to walking to Bulduri and back in search of provisions. Then one Sunday morning Krommer came to Ilgeciem and made her a present of a brand new bike. You can imagine how delighted she was.

Towards the middle of December Uni went on foot to visit our blind friends at Jugli. The roads were a sheet of ice and everybody was tumbling about, and she fell and cracked a rib. It was frightfully painful, but with her usual stoicism she took very little notice of it; only she gave up her room downstairs because she could not lie flat on her camp bed; so ever after she slept more or less in a sitting position on the couchette in the dining room. It was months before she was healed.

On Christmas Eve Dad and Lina had supper with us. Dad brought a bottle of wine and we drank to the health of all our dear ones. We had a tiny Xmas tree in a red bucket. On 28th December we had a Red Cross message from Eugenia to say Rhona was getting married. Great rejoicings! and oh we longed to hear all the details.

Just about that time Charlie Ellis was interned. His wife happened to be out when he was arrested, and it was weeks before she could find out where they had taken him to. It turned out to be the Central Prison. I wrote petition after petition to the authorities, begging them to set him free, because he was past seventy and very ill; but no notice was taken, nor was his wife permitted to write to him or visit him. It was a very severe winter, and his cell was not heated. The water trickled down the walls and he wore his winter coat and fur cap night and day. Eventually he was transferred to the Terminal Prison near Kaiserwald. One day a woman came to Charlie's wife and told her that she had seen him being led by a gaoler from one prison to another, a long way off, on foot. Charlie kept stopping every minute to get his breath (being in an advanced state of heart disease). The old woman asked him why he did not take a taxi. He said he had no money. Then, though she was quite a stranger, she lent him fifty Marks, and he gave her Olla's address. The old woman told Olla he was looking very ill.

On February 10th 1942 the so-called *Sicherheitspolizei* came and searched Dad's rooms for firearms and compromising documents; found nothing; arrested Dad and carried

53

him off. As he passed our door he opened it, waved his hand, and smiling called out, 'So long!' We were terribly upset, and poor Lina was quite stunned. The next day she went to the *Prefektura* and saw him (at a distance) sitting on a hard bench with Mrs Francke and Miss Harrison. Lina took him a blanket and some toilet necessaries, but was not allowed to speak to him. She quite broke down when she got home. Dad spent four days and nights in that filthy place, sleeping on the floor, and eating black bread and so-called soup, just dishwater with bits of cabbage-leaves floating around. From that place he was marched off between two policemen, like a convict, through the town to prison, his only crime being that he was a British subject. The cell he occupied in this prison with sixteen convicts was indescribably filthy, and he was glad when he was transferred to the Central Prison.

One day Uni met an old Bulduri friend, K., who belonged to the Secret Police. He asked after us all, and when he heard that Dad was in prison, he said he would see what he could do for him. So we wrote Dad letters and sent him food through K., and on Easter Monday, the latter arranged a treat for poor Dad. He gave all the gaolers on that floor a holiday, took Dad into his own room, and they had a beanfeast (provided by us) and a jolly good binge. After that K. constantly took him letters, books and parcels of food from us.

Dad wrote back to me, and in one letter which he dated: March 15th *De Profundis* — he said: 'I don't know why you are so optimistic. I feel sure I shall not get out of this till the war is ended.' I replied that Krommer was moving heaven and earth to get him released, and we had great faith in him. Eventually Charlie Ellis was brought to the same prison and shared Dad's cell. Charlie was desperately ill, and was often too weak to get up. He afterwards told me that he had no idea Trevy could be so kind. He nursed him, lifted him in and out of bed, made his bed, tore up his handkerchiefs to bandage his hand, and looked after him like an angel.

One day Dad sent us word that our friend the King of Sweden was dead. He had been arrested in August 1941 while walking to Majori; hustled into a motor car and taken to the Central Prison. It appears that he had been concerned in the

'*Putsch*' against Hitler nine years previously. Being a political criminal he was literally starved to death, and though very ill was denied a doctor or medicine under the Nasty regime. When he was dying he sent us grateful messages, saying he could never forget our kindness to him — and begging us, when the war was over, to write and tell his brother who was *Oberbürgermeister* (Lord Mayor) of Nürmberg of his sad and tragic fate.

Olla Ellis so importuned the authorities that at last they sent two officers to see if Charlie was as ill as she made him out to be. When they saw him they said: 'You must go home at once. We are going to phone to your wife to fetch you immediately.' So off he went and Olla put him straight to bed. I went to see him on the following day. He was looking terribly ill, but ecstatically happy to be home again. Olla too was radiant. He told me about his experiences in the various prisons. Oh, those Huns! — He was released on May 15th 1942. He and Olla came over to Ilgeciem and had tea with us on July 29th and on August 5th, poor old Charlie died. Uni and I went to his funeral. So did Dad and Lina.

Noony had taken Lina to a celebrated fortuneteller some time in March. She said, amongst other things: 'Your husband is away from home, but he will come back quite unexpectedly and you will not be there to welcome him.' And sure enough so it happened. On June 16th I went into the bathroom, and there was Dad, just about to shave. It was such a surprise that I hugged him, a thing I had never done before. Lina had gone down to Bulduri quite early and did not get back till suppertime, and then great was her joy.

My bedroom window at Ilgeciem looks out on Daugavgrivas Street, and a grievous street it is, a street of sighs and bitter tears. I could see the melancholy procession of Russian warprisoners, daily marching to their work at the Aerodrome, and back again to their barracks at the Brewery. A heartrending sight it was. Most of them so worn-out with hunger and disease, they could scarcely drag their weary limbs along. They

55

were all in rags, with torn boots and often without socks — sheets of paper round their shoulders instead of coats. I remember one man who was wearing a lady's straw hat trimmed with flowers — a grotesque and miserable company. Their escort, the most brutal and savage Huns, bawling at them all the time. Once a Russian prisoner fell down at our gate and could not get up. The Hun kicked him savagely, yelling '*Aufstehen, die Schweinehund!*' The poor victim tried to get up, but fell back again. The Hun, beside himself with rage, seized hold of his legs and dragged him across the street on his face. Just then a car was passing, and the Hun called out to the chauffeur 'Drive over the swine!' The chauffeur stopped his car. Our two watchmen turned away and were sick. Then the wretched moribund was flung on to a cart that always escorted the prisoners. It was full of dead and dying, with their heads, arms and legs hanging over the edge of the cart. The Letts who were looking on at this ghastly scene muttered ' Kulturtauts' and a Russian woman, one of our factory hands, was arrested because she was shedding tears of sympathy. Noony's friend, Arema, a Russian prisoner who worked at Weissenhof and once breakfasted with us, told us that all these dead and dying men were shoved into a shed where they froze to death and there was an accumulation of corpses which would not be buried till the snow melted and the ground thawed in spring.

People were forbidden to feed the prisoners, but Noony often managed to slip a little bread into their hands as she passed them on her bike. Later on quantities of these war-prisoners were made to work in our mill-yard, and I used to give them food surreptitiously. One day when I was crossing the yard a soldier of the Mongol type sidled up to me and whispered 'Is there bread?' I replied, 'Yes'. As I was fumbling in my bag for small parcels of bread and fish he spied the German guard coming and hissed "Hurry up." Then he seized my beautiful work-bag and decamped with it. They were a thievish lot, and would sneak up our stairs and steal food from our store-cupboard on the landing. One morning I was having my bath and a Russian soldier came to the door of the bathroom and asked who was there. 'Go away!' says I. 'What are you doing?' 'Having a bath.' 'What for? How old are you?' 'Eighty-two,' says I. 'Get away!' 'That's a lie, your voice is young.' 'Let me in, I want to see you.' 'If you don't go away I shall call the German officer who lives in the next room (a myth) and he'll shoot you,' whereupon he crept into the kitchen and helped himself to some bread. After a while he came back and asked again how old I was. 'I tell you I'm eighty-two. Go away.' Fortunately just then Uni came along, and I called out 'For the love of Mike rid me of this pestilential fellow!'

Another time we had a dozen pancakes over from dinner; so Uni put them in a paper bag, and we opened the window and saw five prisoners sitting on a bench in the sun. Uni waited till the German guard's back was turned, and flung the bag to them over the hedge. They leapt up and rushed to the spot. The first man sat down on the pancakes, and the rest fell upon him and a furious fight ensued. Meantime the guard turned, and seeing this struggling, heaving mass on the ground, yelled out *'Seid. Ihr verrückt geworden?'* and cuffed them all soundly. The man who had sat down on the pancakes managed to slip them into his pocket. It was really awfully funny.

Another amusing incident happened at Weissenhof (your first home) where Noony was working. One day at the dinner hour two soldiers from the Aerodrome close by brought a barrel containing twenty litres of sour milk for the eighteen prisoners who were also working there. They ate it with great gusto, and just as they had finished the last drop, the soldiers came running back and said: 'It was a mistake. We took the wrong barrel and must take it back immediately. It contained twenty litres of whipped cream for the officers' mess!' You must know that no one except children and invalids was allowed any milk, while the *Wehrmacht* as well as the *Reichsdeutsche* civilians lived on the fat of the land.

Persecution of the Jews

In the autumn of 1941 the persecution of the Jews was started. They were all ordered to evacuate their flats at a moment's notice and to go and live in the ghetto in the Moscow suburb of Riga. Their furniture and most of their possessions were confiscated. They were made to wear the 'Star of David', a large yellow star, one on their breasts and another on their backs. They were forbidden to make use of any public conveyances, such as trains, trams, buses, taxies or steamboats; to visit theatres, concerts, cinemas or circus; to walk on the sidewalk. It did make me furious to see Letts, Germans, and even dogs walking on the side path, while the unfortunate Jews had to march in the middle of the road or in the gutter. On November 25th I received a touching little note from Ina. She no longer studied at the University, but was working somewhere in the Vorburg. When their work was done the Hebrews all formed little groups and were marched back to the ghetto by German guards. I once spoke to a group of Jewesses who were shovelling the snow off the tramway lines. They were attired in light coats and skirts with the thinnest of shoes, and I asked them whether they were not perishing with cold. They replied that they could stand the cold, but oh! the hunger, that was far worse. They said that five hundred of them had been brought to Riga from Cologne. They were told that their husbands and children would follow. They were each to take a suitcase containing their valuables. When they reached Berlin they had to change trains. Porters took their suitcases, and they never saw them again. After that thousands of Jews, men women and children were imported from Germany. Though strictly forbidden, Uni and I spoke to lots of them. There were scores of them working at our factory. Some of them used to slip upstairs and beg for bread, and we often gave them a good meal, and heard many a tale of woe.

Ever since the advent of the Germans many Jews had been killed, but in the autumn the wholesale massacre of the Jews in the ghetto started. They were driven in lorries to the Bickern Woods near Jügli to be killed. The following is an account of proceedings given to Dad by one of the jailers at the Central Prison who had attended many of these executions: In the dead of night, with the thermometer at anything up to −20° or −25° Réamur, the Jews with their wives and children were told to dress in their best for a long journey and to take all their treasures with them, such as jewellery, money, clothes etc.

Having reached the Bickern Woods they were made to get out and walk in single file. First came an order to take off their fur coats and drop them into a long trench; next their coats, waistcoats and pants into a separate trench; the women their frocks — then their underwear, boots, shoes and stockings each into a special trench, and lastly their suitcases with their valuables. Many Jews, he said, when it came to the valuables, chucked their suitcases into the deep snow on the opposite side, and these were dug out and appropriated by the people who lived in that neighbourhood. Then, stark-naked, they had to mount a knoll from which, being shot down by machine-guns, they fell into a deep trench about 100 feet long.

Another eye-witness, a Russian prisoner working at Weissenhof, told Noony that he and many fellow-prisoners had had to dig these immense graves and stand round on guard while the massacring was going on, lest any should try to escape. He said his hair used to stand on end, and he showed her how high his cap was lifted with terror. He said it was so awful to hear the shrieks of those poor victims and to see the naked children, panic-stricken, running about and clinging to his legs for shelter. 'The German soldiers who shot them were given plenty of schnapps, but we got none,' he said. Another man who was compelled to be present at these revolting scenes was Anson, chauffeur to the chief of the Gestapo who presided at all the massacres.

Noony used to meet Garber, our chemist, in a yard where the Jews assembled after their day's work, and take him food, for he was half-starved. He was doing hard work, and as long as he was able to work his life would be spared. His old father of ninety, his mother, sister and two brothers had been slaughtered. He said 'If I could tell you half the horrors I have witnessed!' One day a young woman and her five little children were being led through the streets of the ghetto to be executed. She fainted and they shot her on the spot, and then put bullets through the brains of the five kids; and he, Garber, was made to cart the six corpses away on a wheelbarrow, dig a hole and bury them.

One day Uni met Zig-Zag who told her that Hirschberg, John Thal and many other friends of his had been shot. He himself was safe for the present, because he was useful to the Germans; but for how long? We made enquiries for Ina Shalit and her mother, but were told they were no longer at the ghetto. Olga, the blind girl, used to spend the weekends with her cousin at Bickern. She said it was impossible to sleep for the noise of the machine-guns which went on incessantly from six pm on Saturday till nine am on Sunday. After this had been going on for two years or more we heard that 2000 more Jews had been massacred in one night. Thinking this might be an exaggeration, Olga Mossoloff asked a girl she knew who was working in an office where statistics were kept, and she replied: 'As a matter of fact there were 2500;' and she added: 'I may be wrong, but must say I *cannot* approve of these wholesale executions.'

In order to humiliate the Jews still more all their clothes were taken away and they were made to wear prison garb, the women as well as the men; and the women, whose pride and glory is their hair, had their heads shaven, and a parting made, about three inches wide, from the forehead to the nape of the neck, to hinder them from escaping. They all wore turbans, even on the hottest summer days, to hide their disgrace. Hundreds of these women in turbans passed my window every day. I felt so sorry for them. Mrs Small came to see us one day and she told us she had had a surreptitious visit from a young Jew of her acquaintance who had managed to escape being shot by jumping into the pit before the bullets reached him, and when all was quiet he had struggled out from under all the corpses, many of which were still alive, and had run, stark-naked, to a neighbouring cottage to beg for shelter. The people had been very kind and had provided him with clothes, but they dared not take him in for fear of being shot themselves. So he had made his way to Kaiserwald and implored Mrs Small to hide him. She kept him a night and a day, but she too was too frightened to keep him any longer. (Mr Small had just died, and she was alone, with German tenants on the upper floor.) The things this Jew told her about the midnight massacre of the Hebrews made her hair stand on end. Dad also told us about a Jewish lad of sixteen who had pretended to be dead and afterwards crept out of the pit. He was caught and taken to

60

the Central Prison. Every day he was mercilessly thrashed, and after a fortnight Dad saw him being led away to be shot.

One of the huge glass buildings of the marketplace was packed to the ceiling with confiscated Jewish furniture, the contents of all their shops, fur coats and every sort of thing. The bulk of the goods was sent to Germany; the rest was sold to *Reichsdeutsche* who came and settled down in Riga, usurping all the best posts and cushy jobs. All the shops were shut except the Army and Navy Stores, to which only Germans had access. We were allowed to buy one pair of stockings a year.

A German paymaster, a harmless little squirt, by profession a schoolmaster, begged me to give him English lessons. He came five times a week for one and a half hours and made prodigious strides. He was in charge of the Jews who worked in our factory, and was most obliging in lending us electricians to repair our electric fittings, bricklayers to mend the bathroom stove and a watchmaker to repair our watches. These were all very cultured Jews, talking the most perfect German, and we had many a chat with them. One or two would occasionally sit with Ganf who enjoyed their conversation. The clock-maker had an only child, Alica, aged eight — the apple of his eye. One day I enquired after her and he burst into tears and said that she and her grandmother had been 'liquidated'. Another, Mr Maune from Hanover also had an only child, a boy of five, and he too had been led away to the slaughter. It was dreadful to see his grief and despair, and when I tried to comfort him by saying that his wife, who was only twenty-four years old would bear him more children when the times were better, he only wept still more and said that was impossible, because she had been 'sterilized' like all the women in the ghetto. Aren't they unmitigated beasts?

The paymaster was very kind to the Jews. They said of him '*Er ist ein goldener Mensch.*' Once he came late to his lesson and said he had been detained. There had been a shemozzle among his Jews. One of them had been denounced for selling a valuable ruby ring. They were strictly forbidden to trade. His

61

superior officer had come to Ilgeciem to investigate the matter and find out the culprit; but he could get nothing out of them, because he terrified them so. So the paymaster said: 'You leave it to me and I'll soon get to the bottom of it.' 'Yes, but I must know the truth by one o'clock,' said the infuriated officer as he took his departure. Then the paymaster took the Jews in groups of ten, showed them the ring and questioned them. They first stipulated that they should not be shot nor sent to the Kaiserwald, where they were treated more cruelly than anywhere else. Then one man confessed, and when asked what he had sold the ring for, he said two loaves of bread. ('A terrible crime when one is starving,' I remarked.) He was reprimanded and told: 'This ring belongs to the state.' In the meantime another wretched Jew, having sixty Marks in his pocket had hidden the money in a corner of the room. Another inquisition, and he owned up that it was his money. When asked how he had come by it he said that his old mother before dying (?!) had bequeathed him her eiderdown into which she had sewn a hundred Marks. 'What have you done with the rest?' 'I spent it on bread.' This money too was confiscated and appropriated by the State.

My paymaster also used to tell me interesting episodes out of the campaign in Russia. He had taken part in the siege of Moscow. He spoke of the German retreat from Stalingrad. They were making for the Crimea across the Steppes with the Red Army in hot pursuit. One night a blizzard came on, and they hastily entrenched themselves and lay down to sleep. It snowed heavily all night and in the morning, as far as the eye could reach, not a single enemy was to be seen on the undulating landscape. So the Germans emerged from the trenches and thought they would go off in search of a village or farm in the hopes of obtaining some food. Suddenly, at a given signal, all the undulations sprang into life, and out of each appeared a Russian soldier, fully equipped, who had lain down to sleep and been covered with several feet of snow. The Huns turned and fled hell for leather to their trenches.

This reminds me of a comical incident in the train from Bulduri to Riga. We had stopped at Imantov, and just as the train was about to start again we saw two German soldiers sprinting across the field to catch the train. The passengers all said they would never catch it. But a German general, who was slightly inebriated, said 'I bet you they'll catch it all right. We Germans are good runners. I myself have run away from Stalingrad, from Kiev and from Rostov.' And when the two soldiers actually jumped into the moving train, he said triumphantly: 'There, didn't I tell you so? We Germans know how to run! . . . '

On Saturday January 30th 1943 Dad was taken ill. In the morning he said he felt seedy and would not go to his work. His temperature was 39.5°. By noon it had risen still higher and he was unconscious, and evidently in great pain, tossing about and moaning incessantly. No doctor to be had. He never recovered consciousness. On Sunday morning I met him on the landing in his pyjamas, with bare feet on the icy-cold tiled floor, going into the bathroom, where he shaved quite mechanically and then seemed puzzled as to what to do with his shaving tackle. He was put back to bed. In the evening the doctor came. When he entered the room, Trevy leapt out of bed and stood at attention, as he had had to do in prison when the authorities arrived. It was too pathetic. The doctor diagnosed cerebro-meningitis and ordered him to be taken to the hospital without delay. At ten pm the ambulance arrived, and Lina and Uni accompanied him to the hospital. On the way Dad murmured, 'Where to? and what for?' Lina told him he was being taken to the hospital to get well.

The next morning Lina and Noony went to see him. There was no change and he did not recognize them. The following morning, Tuesday 2nd February, they rang up quite early to enquire how he was, and were told he was passing away; so they hurried off again and when they got to the hospital it was all over. Lina was awfully distressed — the whole thing had been so sudden, she could not grasp it at all, and for days she could not say anything but, 'What is life? what is life?' Just after his spirit had fled Dad was changed beyond all recognition: a little, shrivelled-up old man. Lina wished she had not seen him like that, so that she might have remembered him as he had been only three or four days before. I comforted her and said: 'He will be all right when you see him again tomorrow.' And so he was, looking just his own self, so the last impression was a pleasant one. She was not allowed to touch him, as it appears this kind of meningitis is awfully infectious, and all Dad's belongings had to be disinfected. It was all very sad, and Ganf was very cut up. Mr Krommer came round immediately to offer to help us in any and every way, and lent us his car to go to the funeral. The Bulduri fire-brigade* sent their fire-engine with Eglet and three other men to fetch the coffin from the hospital and deposit it in the Chapel of our little Churchyard at Bulduri. The funeral took place on Saturday 6th February, and the dear old Master officiated. He performed the ceremony partly in Lettish but mostly in Russian. The chapel was beautifully decorated, and all the members of the fire brigade were lined up on either side of the catafalque. And now Dad rests besides little Ting-Ting** and both their headstones say: 'Sacred to the memory of Harold Treveven Hall'.

Then Uni, Lina and I drove home. Ganf was not able to attend the funeral, so we had asked Mr Lawson to keep him company during our absence. For a long time we felt quite lost without Trevy; he was such a tower of strength.

On the day of Dad's funeral, Lina's old mother fell on the ice near the well and broke her leg. She was taken to the hospital in Riga and suffered agonies for three weeks, as she was too old to have the leg set — and pneumonia set in, as it always does in such a case, and she died. Lina nursed her most devotedly, even sitting up with her the last three nights. Poor Lina, she was quite exhausted and still went on asking 'What is life?'

The bloodthirsty Huns now turned their attention to the gypsies, who, they said, were a thievish and good-for-nothing tribe and never did any work. Two hundred gypsies were killed at Tuckum.

The lepers came next. All the inmates of the Leprosorium

* Dad had been honorary fire-chief for years.
**Ting-Ting, Dad's only son, our brother, died at 9 years.

just outside Riga were liquidated. Finally came the lunatics. All the inmates of the two asylums of Rosenburg and Alexander-shöhe were taken to the Bickern woods and massacred in cold blood. Leon Straum's wife who, as you know, had been a nurse at Rosenburg for upwards of twenty years, told me that the ghastly scenes she witnessed at these performances which she was compelled to attend beggared description. Many of the lunatics, suddenly realizing what was happening, seemed to regain their senses and their screams and prayers were heart-rending.

My pupil Boy Blue, after a long absence, came to me one day looking like nothing on earth. He too had had an awful experience. He and two of his school-fellows bought a wireless set and used to listen in to the English news, which of course was strictly forbidden. Boy Blue, knowing the language very well, translated the news into Latvian, and they distributed the leaflets among their friends. Soneone must have denounced them, for they were arrested and thrown into the Central Prison. His two friends were never heard of again — presumably they were shot — but B.B. was cross-questioned, and when he refused to speak was bastinadoed most savagely after which he had to be carried down the stairs to his cell by two policemen, and he did not regain the use of his feet for five days. Three times he was called at three am, thrust into a taxi by a German Commissar accompanied by a soldier with a gun, and the chauffeur directed to drive to the Bickern woods, the scene of all the executions. Then the Hun would say: 'Now perhaps you will tell us what we want to know while we take a little drive?' But the poor devil really had nothing to tell, and so after three weeks they let him go; but he could get no job anywhere, for there was a notice on his passport to say that he had been in gaol.

For two or three years Riga was teeming with Spanish and Italian officers and soldiers, whom Hitler had roped into his campaign against Russia. Hundreds of them lived at the Strand. They were very wild, noisy and undisciplined, a perfect terror to the girls who were never allowed out after six pm.

As for the German soldiers, I must say they were always well-behaved, and most civil and kind to old ladies. They

65

always helped me to get in and out of trams and took charge of my parcels etc. Once I was going to get into a tram, but seeing it was overcrowded and people even standing on the steps, I decided to wait for the next. But two young German soldiers standing on the platform sang out: '*Mutti muss mit!*' I said there was no room for Mutti, but one of them insisted. He said '*Ohne Mutti wird nicht abgefahren!*' and bending down, with his powerful arms he lifted me right up on to the platform, where I could only keep my balance by putting my arm round his neck. I said, 'I wonder what my husband would say if he saw me with my arm round a German soldier's neck.' '*Können Sie ihm rectig erzählen,*'quoth Fritz. The other said '*Mutti wird noch auf ihren Sterbebette scherzen.*' Another time I was sitting beside a warrior in a packed train and two Lettish flappers were elbowing their way past the strap-hangers. A German soldier refused to let them pass until they had said '*Bitte*'. 'Have you never been taught manners?' he said, and he barricaded the door till they muttered '*Bitte*'. I said to my neighbour, 'I want to get out at the next stop, but how shall I get past that fighting-cock?' whereupon he roared out in a stentorian voice: '*Platz gemacht für Omama* (Granny),' and they all jumped aside, and helped me to alight.

One dark winter's evening, Noony was coming back from the Strand laden with parcels. While waiting for the tram she deposited a heavy bag on what she took for the doorstep of a ruined house that had been destroyed by bombs. Instead of the doorstep, however, it turned out to be an open cellar window and the bag went slithering down, down, down into the cavity. She made up her mind to come back in the morning and try to retrieve it. Just then two Fritzes came along and she asked if they happened to have an electric torch. She explained to them what had happened, and they ran right round the house to see if they could get in, and finally slid down into the cellar by the same window and rescued the goods, a bottle of milk, groceries, books and what not which were scattered all over the floor.

Considering Latvia was supposed to be a friendly state and had not been conquered by the Germans who had only come to liberate us from the yoke of the Bolsheviks, and stayed on (ostensibly) to protect us from them — it was amazing how they sucked the country dry. This rich province was drained of all foodstuffs. There was a flour-mill close to us, and day by day I used to watch hundreds of lorries packed with beautiful white flour pass my window on their way to be shipped to the Fatherland. No one could buy even an oz of white flour; we got nothing but rye flour for black bread. The same with butter, eggs, poultry, bacon and apples. As for strawberries, we never saw any during the four years of occupation. They were all requisitioned for the Germans, and a strict watch was kept at all the stations, and anyone carrying a basket of strawberries was fined and the goods confiscated. They also exported thousands of cows. At one time there were 10,000 cows at the Hippodrome waiting to be shipped, and as there were not half enough people to milk them, lots of them died, and the stench was awful.

During the winter of 1942-1943 our rooms were very cold. We had to economize on fuel, because, although we had had a supply that ought to have lasted us five years, the Germans started carting it away in lorries till there was none left. Again Krommer came to the rescue, and sent us sufficient wood to last us two years. Besides that the Germans stole every bit of machinery out of the factory, leaving nothing but the bare walls and the roofs. Then they planned to start a steam laundry for the Wehrmacht, and imported huge boilers which they had looted from some other factory. But nothing came of that plan. They then resolved to supply the army with uniforms, boots etc and put up a huge placard above our gate: *Bekleidungsstelle für die Wehrmacht.* But that too was a washout. At last we asked some of our Jewish friends what they were really playing at, and their reply was: '*Es ist ein Affentheater.* They try one thing after another and accomplish nothing, and the result is chaos'.

67

April 30th 1943 was our Diamond Wedding, and we resolved to celebrate it at Bulduri on the QT. Accordingly on the 29th we hired a one-horse cab to the tune of eighty Marks and Ganf and I drove down to Cariah's. It was perishingly cold and it took us hours to get there; but it was worth it. As we crossed the railwayline at Nordeckshof the faithful Natalie handed us a bunch of roses. One of my pupils, a Lettish lawyer of the name of Grinberg, a brother-in-law of Eric Prehn's, told me that on such an occasion we were entitled to a grant from the Lettish government; so we applied for it and were given flour, butter, sugar, eggs, some pork, wine and liqueurs. Thus we were enabled to bake Kümmelkuchen, Speckkuchen, seed-cake and other nice things and we had a marvellous spread. Uni, Lina and Alide arrived on the morning of 30th and we arranged everything most beautifully. Everybody sent us the most gorgeous flowers: lilacs, roses, tulips, daffodils ... and the drawing room and two verandahs looked very gay. So did the groaning board. We received two telegrams addressed to the 'Diamantenpaar, Bulduri'. The postmaster was much mystified as no name was mentioned, and he sent a boy to enquire from house to house till he found us. At about three pm visitors began to arrive, and each one brought us gifts: fish, butter, a huge cake (Torte), liqueur, more cakes, biscuits and whatnot. All agreed that it was a very elegant feast, and really it was a great success. Ganf was most animated and sweet and thoroughly enjoyed it all. Of course we missed our beloved children, and we toasted you all. Ganf and I thanked God very fervently for allowing us to live together so happily for sixty long years.

Then, instead of returning to Ilgeciem after two days, we agreed to stay on at the Strand as long as possible. My former pupils came flocking around as usual, and five new ones besides, so that I was extremely busy. I used to get up very early and put in two or three hours' work in the garden before breakfast. The weather was mostly fine, and Ganf was able to take all his favourite walks. Uni used to come down every morning, cook our dinner, bathe in the sea, do a million jobs and go back to Ilgeciem in the evening in case of telephone calls from the *Sicherkeitspolizei*. Then after two months those unspeakable Huns turned us out once more with dire threats of internment if ever we transgressed again. We were frightfully sorry to leave, but we had had two rapturous months, and so we meekly returned to Ilgeciem by steamboat, and lived on the memory of that happy interlude. Noony saw us on board the steamer, then biked to town and met us on the quay so as to collect our luggage and put us into a cab.

When Charlie Ellis died I gave Olla leave to bury him in the spot where my parents and my three brothers lie in the Riga cemetery. One day she was tending the graves, when a young man in a brown uniform asked her if she could tell him anything about Alexander Hill (my father) and all the other Hills in the churchyard: Nicholas Hill, James Hill, and others. Olla said she knew nothing about the family and referred him to me. He came to Ilgeciem and introduced himself as Dr Eric Wheeler-Hill. He said he had just come from Germany and had visited his grandfather's tomb, a certain Thomas Wheeler-Hill, who, I told him, had been buried by *my* grandfather about ninety years ago. He wanted to know whether he was related to any of us. I told him I was positive we were not related to the Wheeler-Hills; but he seemed obsessed with the idea. He had made a list of all the Hills whose names he had read on the tombstones. So I sorted them out for him to the best of my ability and even gave him the names of my father's nine brothers and three sisters. We thought him eccentric, but very pleasant, and we asked him to come again. So he used to drop in now and then for a chat and always brought cigarettes for Ganf. He heard we were going to celebrate our diamond wedding, and not being able to find really beautiful roses in Riga, he found his way to the Darzkopiba* at Bulduri and bought us some exquisite red roses (so Mrs Sparmin told us). He had no idea we had flitted to the Strand, so he took the roses to Ilgeciem and was very disappointed to hear that we had left — and so we never got the roses after all. Later on he visited us with his wife and child, and before leaving for Germany he gave Noony his wife's bicycle which has been a

*The Darzkopiba — Latvian Government Horticultural College.

69

perfect godsend to her, and she gave hers to Lina. Dr W.H. worked out a most elaborate genealogical tree of the Hill family — funny little cuss! I used to call him my long-lost cousin.

Mrs Francke, Miss Harrison and Mrs Foster Anderson had been interned in the Central Prison for two years and were now released. Poor Mrs Francke had first been confined in a filthy cell with thirty women. There were only ten beds, and they slept three in one bed. Mrs Francke's bedfellows were a woman with TB and another with lice. Can you imagine anything more disgusting? Later on they fared better. Miss Harrison who had very bad asthma got into the prison hospital, where the food was much better and there was a very charming doctor. Mrs Francke (according to Sonia) simulated heart disease by jumping on and off the table before the doctor's visit, till she had violent palpitations, so as to be able to join Miss Harrison. She succeeded in her ruse, and they got up a foursome and used to spend their time playing bridge. Mrs Foster Anderson worked in the shoemaker's dept. Uni took parcels of food, books etc to Miss Harrison twice a month and stood in a queue for hours to deliver them. Sonia sometimes stood in the snow six hours with food for her mother. Mrs Francke lived for about a year after her release and then died of cancer at the Red Cross hospital.

I said to Noony one day 'On the 19th of June (1943) I shall be 999 months old,' and on that day she baked me a wee little cake with 999 in sugar on the top. She happened to mention it to the 'Old Dears', with the result that a month later, on 19th July Mrs Tilting, the sister of my *kleine Schülerin,* brought me a cake, (a much larger one) bearing the legend '1000' in sugar. I can have no more such jubilees till I am ninety-two years and seven months old, when it will be 1111; but I hope I shall be dead and gone long before that.

70

The following winter we had a family of Russian refugees billeted on us. They were given two rooms and the use of the kitchen on the ground floor of the Halls' house. I paid them a visit and took them a present. The family consisted of an old man, always referred to as the *xozzuri*. He was a typical Russian peasant, with his hair cut *à la Russe* round an inverted bowl, and the face of a saint; his wife Xenia Antonovna, a dear old body who kissed me on both cheeks; three tall sons and a daughter, Anna. They had three more sons at the front. They all slept in the same room. The mother and daughter in one bed, the three young men in another, and the old man on three wooden stools covered with sheepskin *tooloops* (fur coats). They were scrupulously clean and very religious. They made the sign of the cross before and after meals, and tramped miles to town to attend the midnight mass at Easter in the Cathedral. I offered to lend the old man some books to read, but he said he had his Bible and that was sufficient for him. As a matter of fact he had three New Testaments, and two more he had buried in his garden at home. They told me their sad story. They owned a little farm somewhere near Novgorod. The Germans had looted the farm, stolen their cows, pigs, poultry and food supplies and ordered them to evacuate the place within three hours. They hastily buried the things they could not take away, made up a lot of bundles and they as well as all their neighbours and all the inhabitants of the village were marched off to a station thirty miles off, and every house and barn was burnt to the ground. They were packed into wagons with barely standing-room and were a whole month on their way to Riga. The only relaxation they could get from standing was occasionally kneeling down, and then their feet got trampled on. They brought a goat with them, and whenever we were short of milk, Xenia Antonovna would give us a jug of goat's milk for our coffee. She never let us pay for it. The whole family was employed in the Ilgeciem garden and it was a pleasure to watch them at their work. They toiled ten hours a day without ever looking up from their work — such a contrast to the Letts who spend half their time in gossiping.

I paid them another visit on Easter Day and took them some coloured eggs. The *xozzuri* was, as usual, reading his

Bible. I asked him to read to me. He said, 'What shall I read?' I said, 'Read about the Resurrection.' He then began at the Passion and read chapter after chapter in the most cultured and sonorous voice, till he got to the Resurrection. It took him a whole hour, and I was quite fascinated. He looked inspired.

One day the Un*sicherheitspolizei* (as I called them) came to our dear refugees and arrested the nicest of the three lads. They punched him in the stomach for not answering their questions, which, considering he did not know a word of German, was not astonishing. It appears that he had been employed with a company of Russian prisoners in excavations in the ghetto, and they had come upon a hoard of pre-war Russian gold coins, which they had divided among themselves. He had only received one ten Rouble gold piece, which he had exchanged for German Marks. They took him to prison, but after three weeks he was released.

Before destroying all the beautiful old Orthodox churches in the ancient town of Vishny Novgorod the Germans looted all the priceless images and relics — three railway wagons full — with the intention of transporting them to Germany. The Russians fought for them fanatically. Two wagons were blown up by the Huns, and the third was rescued by the Russians and brought to Riga. Among them was a marvellous, miracle-working image of our Saviour, supposed to have been painted by St Luke. It was put up in the Cathedral on the Esplanade in Riga, and thousands of the faithful flock to it daily and prostrate themselves before it. The priests from Pskov and the celebrated Monastery of Petchora also fled to Riga, and amongst them is a wonderful preacher who attracts crowds to the Cathedral services by his eloquence. He says that his parishioners at Pskov were god-fearing, religious people, but that the people of Riga were wanton pagans compared with them.

Four thousand children from Russia came to Riga, many of them in rags and tatters or just wrapped up in sheets or blankets, their parents having been sent to work in Germany. They were temporarily housed in a Russian Convent, and an SOS was broadcast for people to adopt them. The appeal was immediately answered, and I know of three cases in which these poor infants found happy homes. My friend Vera Africanovna Taboolskaya took a little girl of five and is bringing her up with her own children. They all love her. After Nadia had been with them for about a year, suddenly her parents turned up, having been sent back from Germany to work in Riga. They had found out where Nadia was and were very grateful to the Taboolskys for giving her such a good education. They agreed to let Nadia spend each Sunday with them, and were much amused at the child teaching them table manners and deportment. They told Vera Afrikanovna of the horrors they had witnessed in Russia; how the Germans had burnt down all their houses, many with people in them, and the man burst into tears and said that to his dying day he would never forget the shrieks of his mother and sister being roasted to death. Machine guns guarded the doors, lest the victims should escape.

Mrs Foster Anderson has just been to see us. We asked her to tell us of her experiences at the Central Prison. Amongst other things she told us about a very sweet girl who worked in the shoe department with her, and with whom she had formed a friendship. This girl told her that she was a Jewess, and that she, her mother and two sisters were taken to the Bickern woods one night along with several hundreds of Jews and Jewesses. When they alighted from the lorries they were made to walk in single file on a narrow path between a row of German soldiers with rifles on one side and a row of Lettish on the other. There was a young officer present who rubbed his hands together in ecstacies and said: 'What a marvellous organization! Everything fits in so beautifully.' They were ordered to take off their garments one by one as they walked through the snow and hand them to the soldiers to be thrown into the appointed trenches. After divesting herself of her chemise she took off her rings and mechanically handed them to a German soldier; but he averted his head, and the tears were running down his cheeks, so she dropped them on the ground. Stark-naked they had to walk on to the edge of the grave. Then they were shot down with machine guns. She was wounded in the neck and in the side and jumped into the pit with the rest. She lost consciousness but eventually came to and managed to scramble out from underneath the corpses and to crawl away on all fours accompanied by a boy of fourteen who had also wriggled out of the pit. They managed to reach a little pile of clothes, under which they hid till all was quiet. The German guards were asleep, having been plied with schnapps, and the others, Russians and Letts, were busy pouring quick-lime into the grave. Finally they managed to put on some of the clothes that were lying there and they walked miles till they got to Riga. The girl tramped about for three days and nights without food or shelter, till she was so exhausted that she gave herself up at the police station. She might have gone to friends, but was afraid of getting them into trouble. She was cross-questioned and she told them a cock and bull story about her husband having been killed in battle and her having come from Russia and lost all her luggage, her passport and other documents — and she was taken to the Central Prison pending enquiry. Twice a week she was fetched to the *Sicherheitspolizei* and cross-questioned again and again, till one day she was examined by an elderly officer who was very kind, and said, 'Look here, my dear young lady, there is something that does not agree in your tale. I have a daughter just your age, and I feel for you and should like to help you, if you would tell me the whole truth.' She said: 'Your soldiers shot badly.' He understood, and she made a clean breast of it. The officer kept his word and saw to it that she was put into a more comfortable cell, given better food and work to do. Still the bi-weekly inquisitions continued, and after many months the poor girl broke down under them and confessed. They took down her statement and compelled her to sign it, and soon after she was led out to be shot in company with about a hundred other victims. Mrs Foster Anderson said the prisoners, who knew what was going to happen, all flocked to the windows to see them pass, but she buried her face in her pillow and wept bitterly.

Once while Cariah was spending the weekend with us at Ilgeciem her house was broken into by German soldiers headed by an officer. Minna watched them, but was powerless to interfere. They took all her coats, dresses and linen, her food supplies and even some furniture, leaving the house in an indescribable state of confusion. As these soldiers were quartered in a neighbouring house, Cariah lost no time in bearding the officer in his den and accusing him and his men of stealing her things. He denied everything, but she said 'Why, the chair you are sitting on is mine, and so is that other one! I insist on your returning them at once!' and he did so; but of course the other things were gone beyond recall.

You will have followed the progress of the campaign against Russia on the wireless, the same as we did. You will recollect Hitler's triumphal progress through the Ukraine, the Crimea and the Caucasus. The pride and arrogance of the Germans at all their achievements knew no bounds. The Führer boasted of his conquests and vowed that he would never give up one inch of the territory that he had taken. He also declared that there might be a famine all over Europe, but Germany would never starve. (No wonder, if he had pillaged every country as he had the Baltic provinces.) But when in his boundless conceit and megalomania he dismissed his more prudent generals and assumed the supreme command of the *Wehrmacht*, the turning-point came and he suffered reverse after reverse. The worst one was at Stalingrad, which was taken and retaken by the Russians after fierce fighting. Hitler gave out that the German garrison had heroically defended Stalingrad to the last man, whereas the truth was that 90,000 men, including a Field Marshal and fifteen generals surrendered and were taken to Moscow from where they daily exhorted their comrades in arms to cease fighting for Hitler and lay down their arms; not only by wireless, but by leaflets, signed by all the fifteen generals. Every town and village the Huns were obliged to give up they left in ruins, driving the population before them. They set fire to the houses and crops as they went along till there was nothing left but charred debris.

Hitler paid two flying visits to Riga in order to impress the garrison to hold it at all costs, and severely reprimanded the officers for their negligence and riotous living. As the danger of the approaching Red Army grew nearer the civil population of *Reichsdeutsche* in Riga were gradually repatriated, and great was the confusion on all the railway lines. Then came more processions of peasants from Livonia, all of which passed my window; ceaseless streams of women and children with their horses, cows and sheep, all bound for Germany by way of Bolderaa, Libau and Windau. The women were in tears, having lost their homes and their men-folk. You may believe the Huns were more unpopular than ever. The most amazing thing was the way they kidnapped all the young men and girls in the streets. They formed them into groups, bicycles and all, and rushed them to the quay where steamers were waiting to take them to the Fatherland — without coats or hats or any luggage. Our young friend Mufor was seized too. His father had just died and he had come to town to get a coffin for him, and in spite of his protestations he had to join the glad throng that was marching along and was locked up in the Circus for the night. However in the morning an inspector came round, a man with more decent feeling than the average German, and on being shown the death certificate released Mufor, as well as thirty boys whose protests were equally well founded. They also collared labourers with all their tools, and even a chimney-sweep with his paraphernalia of ropes and brushes. Our Natalie was working in her potato-patch at Nordeckshof when a car drew up, two Germans jumped out and seized her and forcibly shoved her into the car, saying: 'We need workers like you!' Screaming and protesting she was carried off. Poor Natalie was in despair. After they had driven a long way and were passing through a forest, she suddenly shrieked: 'Oh, I have such a stomach-ache, let me out, let me out!' They stopped and waited for her to come back, but she hid and then ran home. It took her four hours to get home, and in the meantime her house had been broken into and looted. Her clothes, crockery, kitchen utensils, her winter supply of potatoes — all gone!

One morning at five o'clock Xenia Antonovna burst into my room, fell on her knees beside my bed and sobbed 'Lucy Alexandrovna, we have got to leave this house tomorrow. They

76

are sending us to Germany. Woe is me!' She hastily killed her beloved goat, and roasted it and made soup for the journey, and gave us a piece too (and jolly good it was, as we had not seen any meat for months). I went down to take leave of them all and gave them little keepsakes and then we watched the sad procession starting. Later on while I was giving a lesson one of the lads came into my room, tore his shirt open and showed me his chest, all lacerated with a knife. He said: 'I have been trying to kill myself, because I don't want to go to Germany!' All the Russian refugees and prisoners were evacuated. All these foreigners imported to the *Reich* were made to dig trenches madly since Göebbels had declared a *Totalkrieg* and was determined to keep the Bolshis out. How futile this forced labour turned out to be!

A friend of Noony's called Margherita who lived in the Terbata iela, when the kidnapping of boys and girls was going on, locked herself into her room and did not venture out into the street for several days, and watched from behind her curtain the extraordinary scenes that were being enacted there. A few days later when the Germans were fleeing helter-skelter from the wrath to come, there was a frantic rush for all the shops and stores, and Margherita saw a very funny scene. Just opposite her window is the Vieniba, a store packed with provisions intended for the Germans. The mob broke into it and fell upon the goods, and terrific battles ensued, '*Mord und Totschlag*' [Murder and Homicide], as she expressed it. One man shouldered a case of butter, whereupon a dozen harpies set upon him, smashed the packing case and scooped up handfuls of butter. The man only retained a small quantity which in its turn was grabbed by a woman. This made him so savage that he seized the butter away from her, dumped it on her head and smeared it all over her face. At that moment a motor car stopped in front of the store, and three Russian officers with cameras leapt out and took snapshots of the comical scene.

But I am getting ahead of my story ... Some time before this the citizens of Riga had been ordered to evacuate the town and to go either to Germany or to Courland. Thousands chose the latter alternative, and once more there was an exodus on a large scale. Some of them, repenting their folly, returned to

77

their flats, only to find them absolutely empty. Alide's nephew and niece went to Polsen, taking Bellow with them. Alide refused to go further than Talsen and then decided to come home. But her house had been nationalized and she is now living with us, having lost everything.

To add to their crimes the Huns stole all the tugs, steamers and rowing boats. The yachts and motor boats (including Dad's) had been commandeered long ago. So that when the bridges were blown up we were quite cut off from the town, except for extemporized rafts, which were very dangerous.

Then the air raids began. We were afraid our house might be hit, owing to the proximity of the Aerodrome, which was the chief objective of the Russians. So we packed our clothes, our linen and our Lares and Penates in holdalls and hid them in the bushes where they lay intact for weeks, till our Russian refugees had dug a shelter for us in the garden. It was a splendid shelter and we transferred our things to it, and when there was an alarm we would hastily dress and go down into it. It reminded me of a third-class railway carriage, and we shared it with the gardener and his family, the office staff and the Russian refugees, and we chatted cheerfully in four languages. Ganf took it perfectly calmly and we got quite used to hopping out of bed, sometimes two or three times in one night, dressing, taking up our suitcases and finding our way to the shelter in the dark. But when it got too hot and the alarms too frequent and the danger of the shrapnel too great, Uni and Lina arranged a private shelter for us, a woodshed under the stairs, where we felt equally safe. As the Red Army drew nearer and the air raids fiercer and more frequent, Uni rigged up beds for us and Ganf and I spent four nights in the cubby-hole under the stairs. Most of our windows were smashed, and the rooms were cold and draughty. Lina made up a bed for herself on the floor in the hall, just outside our door, while Noony never moved from her couch in the dining room.

Three days before the Russians broke through into Riga, Noony offered to take charge of a cow belonging to a farmer who provided us with milk, as the Germans were stealing all the cattle. He was very grateful, and so Uni fetched the cow in the evening and led her through devious paths in the woods to Ilgeciem. It was no easy task. The Aerodrome close by was blazing, bombs were flying and the cow was scared stiff. Twice Noony was challenged by the German sentry and asked where she was taking the cow to. She replied that she was taking her to the meeting-place at the Ilgeciem market, whence they were all starting for Courland at nine pm. They let her pass, and at ten she arrived safely, leading the recalcitrant beast, which had led her the deuce of a dance. Lina undertook to feed and milk her, and she was a perfect Godsend to us and to many, as we shared the milk with the gardener, the two watchmen, our charlady and others, keeping plenty for ourselves.

Two nights later, the Red Army being about to break through the last defence-line, the Germans blew up all the public buildings, such as the War Office and the Gewer-beverein, the Hotel de Rome (near the University) and, worst of all, the electric plant and waterworks at Kegum, leaving the whole town and all the suburbs in darkness and without a water supply. The whole quay, as well as the coldstores, Customhouse and Elevator had been mined and when they blew up the detonations were terrific. We had a grand view of the fireworks from our windows. Three kilometres of hangars at the Aerodrome were blazing, oil and petrol exploding. The flour-mill next door to us was set on fire, and the conflagration was terrifying. Had the wind been a point more in our direction, nothing could have saved our house and factory. For two whole days and nights we were under cross-fire. The Germans had a heavy battery on the Kuckucksberg and another on the island of Kiepenholm close to our yard, while the Russians held Mühlgraben and the Schirtzengarten, and all the shells shrieked and whizzed over our roof, five actually landing in the grounds. There was no sleep to be had that night in that inferno, and it was nothing short of a miracle that we escaped unhurt. We knew our darlings were praying for us. Ganf and I sat hand in hand and thought it would not be so bad if we could both go together. At dinner the preceding day, at the height of the bombardment, Ganf thumped the table and said furiously: 'Damn it all, they shouldn't be allowed to make such a filthy noise. You can't hear yourself speak!'

On 12th October 1944 the Red Army took Riga and two days later they crossed the river and took Thorensberg, Hagensberg and Ilgeciem and the Aerodrome.

Early in the morning of Sunday October 14th the watch-man came up and told us that the Huns had hastily decamped in the night, leaving quantities of equipment, cooking utensils etc behind; and he advised us to go and snaffle whatever we could. The first things Uni and Lina annexed were two tin hats which they donned at once, as a frightful air raid was going on at the time. I went too to see what I could snaffle, and having no helmet I took refuge under roofs whenever things became too hot. It was awfully exciting. In one large kitchen the table had been laid for supper with bowls of soup all untouched, so precipitate had been their flight. There were quantities of pots and pans, bowls, mugs, dishes etc, things that we had not been able to get for years for love or money. There were mountains of excellent brown bread, of which Uni and Lina brought home countless sacks. It was the only bread we had for a whole month, and we fed the cow and the rabbits on it too. Matches galore, writing-paper, electric bulbs ... One of the factory buildings contained 27,000 pairs of straw slippers which, besides being very useful for wearing in rain and snow and about the house, served us for fuel when we were short of wood. I made only one predatory excursion, whereas the others went backwards and forwards many times, till we had a whole roomful of loot. It was great fun getting back some of our own from the Germans who had robbed us of so much. After that the gates were stormed and the mob surged in and looted, not only the things the Germans had left but all the produce of our vast garden as well. The poor gardener was weeping and wringing his hands to see himself and his family left without any vegetables for the winter after all his toil.

At about eleven am on that Sunday morning a party of Russian officers came in and searched the house for hidden Germans. They were delighted to meet their allies and we offered them coffee, and they sat and talked. One of them was a Cossack. He was rather tight and kept making uncomplimen-tary remarks about the British. His aide-de-camp said 'Hush, this is an English house!' 'Ax', said he, 'a treacherous nation.'

80

After them came several other parties of officers. They all wanted to see 'the Mother'. They gave us a Russian newspaper, a little rag about six inches square, with a flaring headline in red lettering: 'Death to the German robbers!' We hoisted the British flag. It was relief to be able to sleep quietly without bombs or alarms.

The Red Army then continued its march towards Windau. They met with fierce resistance all the way to the Strand, the road being mined and deep trenches dug across it. In two days they reached Bulduri. As the bridges were destroyed there was an artillery duel across the Aa, while the Russians brought up their pontoons. They also crossed in ducks, and soon had the Germans fleeing. Dad's house, which was occupied by German soldiers, was hit by a bomb in the upper storey, and so were Sand's, Kruse's and others. A bomb fell in Cariah's garden and killed a German soldier. All her windows were smashed, and she would have been killed too, had she not thrown herself down on her face and lain still till the show was over.

The Germans made a stand at the Lido in Edinburg, and again at Meluzi. *En passant* they blew up the station at Bulduri. They held Kemeri for a long time and were still just beyond Schlock at Christmas. Eventually they established a permanent position this side of Tuckum and the Russians, though they made twelve fierce assaults, were unable to dislodge them. The Germans occupied the line Tuckum—Windau—Libau till peace was signed. It is said that they kept 250,000 men there because Göebbels had promised them that V3 (presumably the atomical bomb which they were grasping for and just missed discovering) would put England out of action, and then they would return to Riga to make Courland a base for further operations. In the end this mighty army and forty generals were obliged to surrender.

One day a female Commissar came round to put us through a catechism. She seemed satisfied with our answers and said to Ganf: 'Don't worry. Nobody will harm you. Good people have come.'

We had two more visits from male Commissars, who told us they had had orders to treat us with great respect and if we had any complaints to make we were to apply to them at such and such an address.

The meanest and most devilish stunt of the Germans was the blowing up of the Kegum electric station and the water-works, plunging us into Egyptian darkness and depriving us of wireless and baths for months. Lina and Noony had to fetch water from the Textile factory, a long way off, till at last a well was dug in our garden. Even then it was a labour to carry pails of water up the stairs. On 17th October Noony was on her way to Bulduri, when a beastly little mongrel cur ran after her and bit her twice in the calf of her right leg. She thought nothing of it at the time and went on carrying two pails of water and huge sacks of wood up the stairs for two or three days, till the wound began to suppurate and she developed a temperature and was obliged to lie up. The leg got worse and worse, and Lina searched high and low for a doctor — in vain. Then Noony made up her mind to go to the hospital. I packed her suitcase, and again Lina tried in vain to get a horse and cart to take her to town. No conveyance of any kind to be had. On the twelfth day Lina managed to force her way into the barracks at Ilgeciem, despite the protestations of the sentry that civilians were not allowed entrance, and discovered a surgeon who agreed to come and see Uni. He was splendid and treated the case very skilfully — and presented her with yards and yards of bandage and all the necessary lotions. He came several times and incidentally overhauled Ganf and prescribed for him. He would not take a penny from us either for himself or for the medicines. So I insisted on his accepting a pot of honey, for which he was very grateful. In course of time the terrible wound healed up, still Noony was laid up for six weeks, during which time Lina did all the catering and cooking for us and was most kind and helpful. While Noony was laid up she and I played chess a great deal, as many as six or eight games a day. We had begun in March 1943, and in the course of eight months we played 1015 games, of which Uni won 450 and I 565, so that I was 115 games ahead. I had lost all my eighteen pupils, except Mme Mossoloff, who came through thick and thin, walking all the way from town and back and crossing the river on a raft. The others had all gone to Germany, either of

82

their own free will, or compulsorily, being kidnapped.

You cannot imagine how awful the darkness was. We had neither lamps nor candles, and from three pm till nine am we groped about in the dark. When it grew too dark for me to read aloud and for Ganf to play patience, I used to snuggle down beside him on the divan and, wrapped up in rugs and shawls, for it was bitterly cold, we used to take imaginary drives in our car for an hour or so, and then he would lie down on his bed till supper-time. If I forgot Ganf used to say, 'Isn't it time for our drive?' Mrs Irbe occasionally sent us a few stearine candles which we lit just for an hour every evening, while we were having supper and washing up. It was an awful job for poor Uni preparing supper with no other illumination but matches. She used up a box and a half each time; fortunately she had secured a case of 100 packets (1000 boxes) from the Germans. After supper we made a fire in the dining room stove with straw slippers and boots, some of which having double soles weighed about 5 lbs each, and made a lovely conflagration, writhing and squirming in fantastic shapes. We sat round it, talking over old times, till nine pm when we groped our way to bed. We missed the news and the music dreadfully.

On 1st December 1944, we made up our minds to try and get down to Bulduri and live in Dad's house, which had been occupied first by German civilians, then by the Wehrmacht and was now occupied by the 94th regiment of the Red Army. The factory had been turned into a hospital and the staff seemed very anxious to have our house. So we suggested to the Haranbruk, who was of the Hebrew persuasion, that we would let him have the house, provided he gave us enough lorries to transport our funiture to Bulduri. He said he would let us have four lorries. I said that was not half enough for the contents of our four rooms and Lina's two rooms, besides the firewood and five cases of books. But he was adamant and refused to give us more than four lorries. In the end he gave us *eleven*, and I presented him with a pair of silver candlesticks in token of our gratitude.

Next I wrote to the Commander of the 94th regiment, politely requesting him to evacuate the house to make room for his allies. I received a very polite answer saying that, although he had hoped to spend the whole winter in our house, he and his men would clear out by the 14th December.

We accordingly started packing and gradually carried the furniture etc down in the entrance-hall, leaving nothing but the beds and a few chairs, and waited from day to day for the promised lorries. We waited and waited, till at last the Haranbruk fixed on Christmas Eve for us to flit. So on that day we rose early and dressed for the journey, and waited and waited while Lina kept bothering the Jew to hurry up with the lorries. He always had some excuse or other. At last he sent a message to say that we would have to wait till the following day, and if our beds had been taken downstairs we might sleep on the floor. Ganf was wonderful. He never murmured, even at this doleful prospect. The cooking utensils were packed and we had nothing to eat. Then the gardener's wife took pity on us and sent up a dish of delicious Sauerkohl and some black bread, besides three little candles off her Xmas tree to 'lighten our darkness'. It was the strangest Christmas Eve we had ever spent.

Just as we had resigned ourselves to our fate, suddenly at about seven pm the old devil sent word that the lorries were ready, and he put four soldiers at our disposal to manipulate the furniture and to accompany us to Bulduri, and with whoops of joy we crept down in the dark and embarked on our adventure. The day before there had been −15° of frost, and we were very much afraid of Ganf catching cold and having another bout of bronchitis; but God tempered the wind to the shorn lamb, and the thermometer rose to −2°. Wasn't that lucky? Ganf sat beside the chauffeur, *à l'abri du vent*, in one of the lorries. Lina sat outside with the soldiers, and Noony and I got into a so-called closed lorry which had no door. It was so crammed with furniture that there was scarcely any room for us. I sat on a chair where the door ought to have been with my legs dangling in space, while Uni perched high up on I know not what and stretched one leg across the aperture to prevent me from falling out. I was quite sorry to leave the old house which had sheltered us for three and a half years.

It was very weird driving in the dark with our backs to the 'horses'. We had a very hilarious drive. The first thing that happened was that the flagstaff fell on my head with a sickening thud, after which Noony unfolded the flag and hung it outside to the astonishment and mystification of the passers-by and of the traffic control who stopped us to inspect our passports. They were quite excited, thinking we were the vanguard of the British Army. Next a waste paper basket containing two heavy vases crashed down on my long-suffering head. As we passed a farm Lina got down, to buy some milk and in the meantime the soldiers opened her bag and pinched Dad's valuable clock, the one which requires winding up only once a year. I lost my winter coat; but those were very few casualties, considering the darkness and the unusual circumstances of our *déménagement.* We arrived at 9.30. The house was in darkness and unheated. There were 2° of frost in the rooms and there was an inch of ice on the floors, owing to the pipes of the central heating having burst. The cheerful, willing soldiers ran to and fro carrying the furniture and dumping it down in the dining room. Lina soon lit the drawing room fire and Noony fried some eggs, and we sat round eating them by the light of one of our Christmas candles, and we were very, very happy, with the British flag proudly flying over us once again.

PART

3

Bulduri
April 30th 1945

My own darling, beloved, adored little Rhona

Your beautiful letter of February 28th has just arrived having taken exactly two months to get here. It was such joy to see your handwriting — I started reading it aloud to Ganf, but I was blubbering so, I could not read a word; so Noony snatched it out of my hand and read it out to us. We were so touched at all the sweet things you said that Ganf too had tears in his eyes and I could not stop weeping for joy and emotion. Thank you my precious kid for all your love and devotion. We were deeply touched to hear how anxious you had been about us all these years, and how you and Lorna had planned to help us — you darlings! We have been so marvellously protected and spared through all these dangerous times, that I knew somebody was praying for us.

This is the 62nd anniversary of our wedding-day. It does not seem so long since our Golden Wedding. We kept our Diamond Wedding in 1943, and though we sadly missed our beloved children, it was very jolly and quite festive. Having been turfed out of this place by the Huns, we ͏   ne down on the QT in a cab (to the tune of eighty roubles) intending to put up at Cariah's for two or three days — instead of which we stayed for two months till we were preemptorily ordered to quit on pain of being interned. A Latvian lawyer who was taking English lessons with me told me we were entitled to a grant from the Government on an occasion like this. So we applied and received flour, butter, sugar, bacon, wine and liqueur etc so that we were able to bake heaps of Kümmelkuchen, Speek-kuchen, seed-cake and other delectable things and entertain all our neighbours who arrived laden with presents, such as cakes, wine, more liqueur — various fish and what not; the room and the two verandahs were very gay with roses, lilies, daffodils

89

and other flowers — and the groaning boards tastefully decorated and laden with good cheer.

After that we spent nearly two more years at Ilgeciem, where we were really perfectly happy and comfortable. Ganf was marvellous — so resigned and patient, though longing for the seaside. He never once murmured or complained. We used to take our daily walks up to the Kuckucksberg, which is really a lovely park five minutes from the factory. Uni was very homesick for Bulduri. Personally I don't mind where I live, as long as I have my dear ones around me, for my curriculum vitae is the same wherever I am. I clear our bedrooms, wash up after breakfast and supper, read to Ganf three times a day and give lessons. I had eighteen pupils at Ilgeciem for English, German and Italian — eight of them were Russians. Poor darling Ganf is blind in one eye and you can imagine how sad it is for him not to be able to read any more. He was very ill again last winter 1944 with bronchitis and asthma. The Huns fell very suddenly in October, and we resolved to try and get back to Bulduri not to the old house, which is in a filthy condition, doors and windows out and the garden full of tanks and horses and carts — besides being occupied. Dad's house was occupied too, but I wrote and requested the CO kindly to evacuate it, which he did — and we flitted hither on Christmas Eve, arriving *bei Nacht und Nebel* in lorries at nine-thirty pm.

The house had not been heated; the pipes had burst and the floors were covered with ice; but we made a big fire and sat in front of it while Noony and Lina made up our beds on the floor of Granny Hall's bedroom. We are frightfully glad to be here again. Ganf takes a constitutional round and round the garden twice a day; Uni caters for us, cooks for us; works in the garden and does 1000 jobs all day; and I potter about 'the daily round, the common task', give lessons, practise the piano (glad to get it back again) and am more than happy. Not being 'workers' we get *nothing* on our ration cards but 300 gr of blackbread a day each; but three times a week I get a pint of milk (30/-) in lieu of money (I take £1 an hour) for lessons, and other things, such as flour, barley, peas and beans, so that we do not starve. Uni makes the most delicious vegetable soups, and we fill up the corners with potatoes boiled in their skins. We each eat half a dozen potatoes and a slice of dry blackbread for breakfast and a cup of synthetic coffee with milk and without sugar. Cont May 3rd

You dear, darling child, it is too sweet of you to want to send us money, but we have managed very well in every way. Up till 1940 we were receiving monthly remittances from Coutts. These ceased when the Huns came. Then Alide's nephew (*amongst others*) financed us and we never lacked money — which we shall repay when the war is over. Everybody sent us eggs, vegetables and all sorts of things — it was simply marvellous how kind all our friends were. I have been writing a synopsis of our experiences since our correspondence ceased, one for you and one for Lorna, in case we pass away before we meet again.

How sweet of you to suggest sending us parcels via Palestine, darling child; but it will be much easier for you and Cecil to bring us a few things when you come over here, which I hope will be soon. We are simply *longing* to see you. I shall mention a few of the things we need most, and shall send you a cheque to purchase them before you start. Ganf is sadly in need of winter pyjamas (he has summer ones). His look like jigsaw puzzles, they are so patched and darned. The Huns would not allow us to buy a single thing, though there was everything to be had at the Army & Navy stores. Non-Teutons were not even allowed in. Once a year we were allowed one pair of stockings! You can imagine the amount of darning I had to do for all three of us. Uni's socks are a sight! Then I should love to have an overall for gardening in — nice and gaudy; and a pale blue one for Uni; and one for Mrs Sparnin, who is about your size, say lilac flowers on a black ground. She has been so wonderfully kind and generous to us and has helped to feed us these last five years.

You will have had an answer re Dad's will by this time. The Huns pinched everything he had, beginning with the factory, his yacht — everything, and so it was difficult for him to make a will, as he was in prison and was only allowed five minutes with his lawyer. So he left all his worldly goods to Lina, knowing she would do the right thing. So Lina made a will, dividing everything in three parts, for Lorna, you and herself. She is the most unselfish person I know except Noony. As for us, you need not think of sending us money, darling. We are getting monthly remittances from Coutts; but the sum we received from the bank every month till 1940, and which was sufficient for all three of us, now only suffices to buy three sacks of potatoes and *nothing else*, owing to the rotten rates. So we are trying to get more funds. We are infinitely touched at your anxiety to help us. God bless you my Treasure. Give my love to Cecil (I don't know what to call him) and much tender love and many kisses to your precious self,

from Mummy, Ganf and Noony.

Bulduri
June 10th 1945

My own darling, beloved little Rhona

We are thoroughly enjoying the summer in this lovely house —
and Ganf walks round and round the garden three times a day,
doing two or three kilometres each time. Noony and Lina work
like niggers in the garden. They have planted myriads of tomatoes, peas, potatoes and every sort of vegetable; and it *is* a job
watering them all, because we have had hardly any rain. I can
only weed the herbaceous border; by reason of my tender age
(as the catechism says) I cannot garden as much as I used to.

I wonder, darling, if Cecil could kindly make enquiries
concerning two Lettish youths: Elmars Remes and Egil
Mezitis. Their weeping mothers beg me to find out if possible,
whether they have been taken prisoners by the British. They
were both kidnapped by the Germans and presumably forced
to join up. I should be very grateful to my dear grandson if he
could obtain news of them. You cannot think how I am longing
for you both to come over to see us. It would give Ganf a new
lease of life.

Noony was at Schlock last Monday and she saw Sophia,
who was looking very fit, and well fed and groomed. She too
would love to see you. Let me know how soon you will be able
to come. All your Latvian friends keep asking for news of you;
they would be tickled to death to see you again. I am longing
for details of your courtship — how and when you first met
your husband, and whether he proposed to you or vice versa?
You asked me to let you know that things I wanted most. My
silk chemises are in rags, though mended and patched and I am
reduced to wearing a slip which gets washed overnight.

Cariah died a month ago of a heart attack. She had been
wonderfully active for her age (eighty) and had walked long
distances up to the last. She was taken ill quite suddenly on
17th June, and as it was unthinkable that she should stay alone
in her house in that state, we brought her here and Uni and I
nursed her for five days — and on 22nd she passed away in her
sleep.

93

I am sorry you have had such bad weather ever since April. Here we have had enough sunshine to last us for several years. Day after day, all May, June and July (with a few exceptions) we had blue sky and gorgeous sunshine; and three times a day I wrote 'brilliant' in Ganf's weather report, which I now keep. Ganf has been able to sit basking in the sun on and off all day — we have sat in the garden which we love and had afternoon tea there and I have been able to read to him (without glasses) till ten pm most evenings. Now, for the last few days, the weather has broken up and we have had a series of thunderstorms and torrential rain. Our kitchen garden is splendid, thanks to Noony's and Lina's unceasing toil. We are enjoying our own vegetables — and hope to have a sufficient supply for the whole winter. Such a crop of potatoes! 350 tomato-plants — tobacco (for Ganf), pumpkins, peas, haricot beans, broad beans, carrots, beetroot, and what not. Scarcely a day passes without our getting presents. Yesterday a farmer's wife presented us with a litre of milk, and at the same time a former pupil of mine brought me a basket containing cherries, cheese, giant cucumbers and tomatoes; a huge piece of birthday Kringle; half a loaf of black bread. Another pupil brought me five kilos of coffee (synthetic) so there is not much danger of our starving. We keep poultry too — so we have eggs and an occasional roast fowl. We get nothing but black bread on our ration cards, because we are not workers — but we manage to get along spendidly. We are longing for curry — you must bring us some when you come. We are everlastingly grateful to the British Embassy in Moscow for forwarding our letters to you.

God bless you my Treasure.
Your loving and devoted Mumsy

Lucy Addison

Sunday

Bulduri
32 Vienibas Prosp
September 2nd 1945

My darling, precious little Rhona

I am so longing to see you both — and I pray every day that you may come soon. We are not getting any younger. Ganf will be eighty-six next Friday, and diddle Mum is eighty-four and a half; so try your damnedest to come soon, my Treasure.

I now have two Russian officers for English lessons; they are very keen and it is a pleasure to teach them. That makes eight pupils.

Alide is with us again, so that Noony's work is not so heavy, and good old Minna comes every morning to wash up and do odd jobs. We have had a gorgeous summer, as much sunshine as we could wish for, but the last few days have been quite autumnal, showery and squally and quite cold. Still we may have an Indian summer to end up with.

Your loving and devoted Mummy

Lucy Addison

My own darling Rhona

There is going to be an Exhibition at the Agricultural College in Bulduri; and we have been asked by the Director Sparnin to exhibit some specimens of our marvellous potatoes, some of which weigh nearly 3 lbs each. They are most delicious, and you would love them. One potato is quite sufficient for a meal for each person. We eat them three times a day. Noony's kitchen-garden has been a great success, and she has planted four beds of strawberries for next year.

Ganf still enjoys his daily walks to the shore. It is awfully funny the way he talks in his sleep. We have long conversations every night. Last night he said 'When are you going to bathe?' I said 'at five.' 'That's too late.' 'Shall we say at twelve? Are you going to bathe too?' 'I don't know — not if it is as windy as yesterday. Anyhow it's too cold for Pooney.' 'Why do you put it into my head?' says I, 'I wasn't thinking of bathing.' 'I wasn't talking to you. I was talking to Drishans (who has been dead twenty-seven years).'

Love to Ches from us all and lots to your sweet self

from loving and devoted Mummy

Lucy Addison

Darling beloved Rhona

Quite unexpectedly I have an opportunity of sending off my memoirs to you. I hope they will interest you, and you will excuse a few discrepancies in the beginning when I had no notes to guide me and may have got muddled in the dates. Two men from the British Embassy in Moscow gave us a surprise visit and they have brought us clothes and food and papers and great joy. They are staying to dinner. Alide who has lost her house and everything is with us. Lina helps at the various farms round about, threshing, digging up potatoes etc. She is marvellous, and gets foodstuffs in return. They (the men from Moscow) say it is not advisable for you to come just now darling. The route is very roundabout and you would have all your luggage and money stolen.

Many kisses from your adoring

Mumsy

Tuesday

My darling Treasure

Please when you come bring me a Catalogue of Dobbie's —
Seedsmen, Edinburgh — and some packets of Nasturtiums
mostly 'Gold Gleam' and any new sort, red ones etc. Also some
antirrhinums and aster seeds — and above all *Vegetable
Marrows*, some ordinary ones and also a few ornamental, star-
shaped ones. *All from Dobbie's.* Darling we are also dying for
curry and a tiny pot of marmalade. I also want two or three
needle-cases. I hope you won't mind my bothering you, my
love.

    They are just off so I must close (two dear men from
Moscow).

                          God bless you my Angel
                          Your own loving

                          Mumsy

Wednesday, Boxing Day

My own darling beloved little Rhona

We spent the day very peacefully and happily. We listened to the King's speech and had a very good programme on the wireless. As often as not the electric light gives out and then we sit in the dark and play intellectual games. Ganf made 110 words out of 'comfortable'; and Uni plays tunes on the violin in the dark, and so the time passes, and just as we get into bed the light goes up.

I should be everlastingly grateful to you my love if you would get me these things and I shall pay you as soon as I can get a cheque-book. What I want most of all is a boudoir cap; mine is ten or twelve years old and I can't do without. Also a few needle-cases. I hate bothering you, but just one more petition. If obtainable I should like two slabs of Fry's chocolate cream — and one or two little chiffon scarves. I had better stop before you begin to curse your Mumsy for a greedy old beast. Have you joined the glorious company of the unemployed? or are you just taking a rest?

Tenderest love hugs and kisses
from your devoted, loving Mumsy

Ganf still has bronchitis; but he gets up every day. He sends heaps of love.

My own darling, precious child

My first letter in the New Year shall be to you. With all my heart I wish you and your dear husband a Happy and Prosperous 1946 with health and wealth and every blessing. May all your wishes be fulfilled, especially that of your visit to your old home and your old folk who are longing to see you again. I wished Noony a happy New Year and the fulfilment of all her wishes just now and she said: 'I have but two wishes: Rhona's visit, and new tyres.' Ganf is also counting the days till you come. The poor old darling has no sweets. Only Lina. But we were happy and peaceful and enjoyed the radio and the King's speech. I had a little sort of exam for my small pupils, five children. They had to do all their stunts, such as spelling with cardboard letters, reading aloud, reciting etc and Mrs Fish came and helped them to sing their nursery thymes and dance round the Mulberrybush and Ring o' Roses. Then they played hide and seek — ending up with coffee and buns and each a bowl of 'bubbert'. They got little presents too, and I think they enjoyed the show. I do want to ask you to try and get a game called 'Happy Families' — Mr Bones the Butcher, Mrs B the Butcher's wife, Master B and Miss B etc. It would be a splendid thing for the children. Perhaps Dorriecorrie could help you to get it. If it is out of date perhaps there is something like it to be had.

> God bless you my Treasure.
> Think of Mumsy when you look at the ring.

Hugs and tender kisses from your loving Mumsy

My beloved, darling adored little Curly-Locks

What a red-letter day was yesterday! After months of silence six letters — three from you and three from Lorna, besides twelve lovely snapshots of you. Again senile tears prevented me from reading them myself, and so Uni kept us spellbound for more than half an hour reading them out loud. She read yours again to me this morning, as I was too excited to take in all the contents at once — so excited, indeed, that I lay awake all night thinking of you and Lorna and never dropped off to sleep till six-thirty am. But I did not mind, for I was warm and comfortable and my thoughts were pleasant and my heart full of gratitude to God for hearing all my prayers.

Poor Ganf has had another bout of bronchitis and has not been able to get out for a walk for weeks; but now he is all right and only the bad weather keeps him indoors. The whole place is a sheet of water with ice at the bottom. Darling Uni has been laid up for three weeks with acute muscular rheumatism of the joints of her wrists. It was sad to see her with her hands all cramped up, unable to move her fingers. She lay in this little sitting room all the time, very patient, but very bored. Mrs Paigle gives her massage. She is splendid. As soon as Uni was able to move the fingers of her left hand we started playing chess. We are pretty even now. It is such a fascinating game, the King of games. You should learn to play it. Before she fell ill she used to play the violin to us when the electric light failed and we had to sit in the dark. Since Sunday Uni has been able to go out again. She has to wrap up very warmly.

Alide is a perfect Godsend and so devoted to Noony. She cooks us such lovely meals. On Sunday she made us a wonderful hot-pot with a minimum of meat, masses of turnips and gravy and crowned with our marvellous, huge potatoes. It was a dish fit for the gods. There is a cock crowing outside the window, which reminds me that we keep some fowls, and they are at present floating around in the garden.

I must not forget to mention how splendid Lina is when

101

Noony is *hors de combat*. She does all our catering, stands in queues, goes miles for milk for us. She is a most unselfish person. She has to provide for Minna and her aunt too. She has most of her meals at the aunt's; but often joins us at dinner or supper. She goes to the doctor for us to get the needful prescriptions, and then to the chemists for medicines. All that is not so easy as it used to be.

You say I look thin on my photo. There was a time, the first year we lived at Ilgeciem, when I lost weight, very rapidly, when our meals were scanty. My tummy, which had been rotund, as you know, shrivelled up and hung down like an empty bag. (*Please* this is for your private ear) and flapped against my legs when I walked. One evening when Lina was very blue after visiting Dad in quod, and Noony was trying to cheer her up, I went into her room and pranced round and round her table, my tummy going flap, flap! till Lina and Noons were in hysterics. Lina would not believe that I hadn't tied a hot water bottle round me, till she felt me all over; and ever after that when I was crossing the landing and they were in the kitchen, they would sing out; flop, flop! I went to the Blind Asylum and the blinds were horrified. Julchen said it was *als ob man Pfannkuchenteig klopft*! By this time I have filled out again and only when I sit down there is a gurgle something like a deflated tyre.

Love and kisses from Ganf and from Noony, who cannot write comfortably yet.

My beloved darling Rhona

We are having bitterly cold weather too; *à l'heure qu'il est* there is a fierce blizzard going on. We have been having them every day, and consequently mountains of snow. We employ two people to keep the pavement swept in the three streets that surround our grounds, and Lina does the inside paths while Noony is *hors de combat.* I wear three pairs of stockings (one of them worsted) two pairs socks, knee-caps and felt slippers lined with fox-fur, and yet my feet are like lumps of ice.

I hope you will be very successful in your new job, darling. How I envy you the possibility of learning Spanish. Though I have studied it and can read anything and everything in Castellano, I have never had any opportunity of conversation. At Ilgeciem I had a pupil for Spanish — a nice little Russian girl. When she asked me for lessons I guessed she was in love with a Spanish officer, of whom there were dozens in Riga, fighting for Hitler. So for her first lesson I prepared a passionate love-letter in Spanish (besides, of course, the usual *Abfangs-gründe*). I translated it to her and she was delighted, but soon afterwards she married a Russian officer and dropped the Spanish.

                    Fondest love, hugs and kisses
                    from your loving, yearning Mumsy

Noony has gone to town today for the first time for months. She has gone by train, because her hands are not yet strong enough to manipulate a bike on these slippery roads. She still has massage nearly every day; and is getting steadily better. As the weather is milder Ganf has been able to resume his daily walks, which make a pleasant break in his monotonous days. I take a trot too when my lessons are done. My little Russian boy, aged six, is an awful little pickle. He is getting on very well with his English, and has set his heart on living in England where the cows jump over the moon; but sometimes he has fits of obstinacy and refuses to read. Then he goes to the end of the room and rushes at me and tries to butt me in the stomach with his head. He never succeeds, because I catch hold of him by his hair every time.

Uni and I always have two or three games of chess immediately after breakfast, till my pupils come. We both enjoy it tremendously. Ganf lies in bed till twelve-thirty. We dine at two and listen to the news. I usually have two lessons in the afternoon, and in the intervals I read aloud to Ganf. Then we play patience; have tea at five and supper at eight. We listen to the Nüremberg trial every evening. Is it not beyond belief that such devils should exist?

Your adoring Mumsy

Lucy Addison

Bulduri
March 19th 1946

My own darling beloved Rhona

This is my birthday, and the first thing I saw on opening my eyes were two pots of lilies of the valley — Ganf's gift for the 64th time! The first time was the year before we were married, and wherever I have been he has never once failed to remember them. When I was in the Klinik in Berlin with Uni he wired to a friend to send me the lilies of the valley. That was a great day. So many letters and telegrams came for me and while I was out the matron had turned the sickroom into an elegant boudoir — the bed carried out and Uni ensconced on a sofa, looking lovely in a pale blue négligé — a Turkish carpet on the floor, a tea-table with a Japanese tea-service. And then at four o'clock came a procession of white-capped chefs from the confectioners carrying pails of chocolate and whipped cream, a Kringel, a huge Torte and a basket of finger biscuits, and each patient on that vast floor had chocolate and cake instead of the usual coffee and bread. The matron was invited, the Chaplain, and the Neveu Du Monts and Hakens. The matron said they had never had such a festival in the Klinik* before.

Today we are having a spread in the drawing room: Kringel and seed-cake, tea and coffee — and Mrs Sparnin is invited, also Lina, Minna, Lina's Tanting and Alide — and it will be very cosy before a roaring fire.

Fondest love and hugs to your sweet self

from Mumsy

*1907 Una was taken to Berlin for surgery after a severe fall from a horse.

My most precious darling Rhona

Tuesday has come round again, and I hasten to start my seventh Tuesday letter to you, long before breakfast. The house is so quiet, not even Noony is up yet, and Ganf is fast asleep. He does not hear me get up — I move about so softly. I am so happy to be back in my lovely drawing room now that the winter is over. With the morning sun shining in, it is delightful. The piano sounds grand in this room, and I play a good deal. I am now learning a sonata of Beethoven. Today I have five lessons to give, so shall not have much time for practising. Noony has let Cariah's bungalow* and high time too, for else there would have been nothing left of it. Last week the windows (bedroom) were pinched and the night before last actually the steps leading to the verandah. The doors would go next. The worst of it is that the culprit is a friend of mine, a former pupil. Whenever they have a birthday or a namesday they invite me to tea or supper. Of course I can't let on, but it is very awkward. She doesn't know that she has been watched and seen carrying off the goods.

Have you any servants, native or otherwise? I do hope so. We are so thankful to have Alide. She is a treasure and takes such an interest in the house; takes a delight in making us nice dishes, and every month when she gets her old age pension she goes to market and buys us meat; though really we have got quite out of the way of being carnivorous. We are practically vegetarians and thrive on it. Noony, Lina and Alide have started working in the garden, though nothing much can be done while the soil is still frozen. It is barely a fortnight to Easter and I must begin colouring the eggs. I do them all with red ink which, laid on very thin, turns them a lovely pink, and then I paint little designs on them. Lina reads English with me

* It was left to her in Cariah's will.

twice a week. We are now reading Winston Churchill's biography, much too difficult for her, of course, but she enjoys it. She always say 'My vocabulary is limited; but she rambles on when we are at supper, making the same faults every time — never knowing the difference between singular and plural, past or present. Yesterday a pupil brought me two fine fishes which we are going to have stuffed: I don't mean embalmed, but disembowelled, mixed with breadcrumbs etc and stuck back in their skins. The day before, another pupil presented me with some delicious veal cutlets, having just killed a calf. We are wallowing in milk at present, as three of my pupils give me two quarts a week in lieu of money; so that we give lots away to old folks and invalids. I think of the Germans, who would not let us have any milk, and when Uni applied for a small quantity for her aged parents, they said 'What's the good of old people? Let them die.' Evidently they wanted us to be dyed peoples too.

Your adoring

Mumsy

My beloved darling Rhona

I am getting lots of letters from old friends from whom I had
not heard for seven years. Some of them are dyed peoples, as
Lina would say: the Pollock twins, Morrell (do you remember
her?) Harry Bett, Leslie Prehu, Adelaide Pollock, killed by a
bomb — all dyed peoples.

Your adoring Mumsy

My dearly beloved Rhona

Today is the 63rd anniversary of our wedding. Such a lovely
wedding it was, and all the British ships on the river in front of
the Church were decorated with all their flags. My white-
haired uncle led me to the altar where Ully Baby was waiting,
and we heard someone say: '*Schade, solch eine jünge Braut, und
solch ein alter Bräutigam.*' They must have been surprised to see
me come out with a rejuvenated bridegroom. Ganf being director of Loder's sawmill we lived in a wood-yard, and we felt so
young that Ganf called us 'The Babes in the Woodyard'; hence
his sobriquet of Ully Baby. He called me This Babe and himself
the Other Baby; and to this day he always says: Ully Baby has
lost his handkerchief, or whatever he wants. You will think
these are the reminiscences of an old woman in her dotage, and
so of course they are.

Tomorrow is the 1st of May, and the leaves are only just
beginning to show themselves. We are handicapped by the late-
ness of our spring. It is too early to plant or sow anything yet. I
have just had a gardener in to dig up and replant the
herbaceous border which had been so neglected for six years, it
was hideous last summer. I wish Ches were here to help me to
group the perennial plants. I was so disappointed that you
could not get me seeds from Dobbie's. I do love a gaudy border
of Golden Gleam nasturtiums. There are very few flowers to
be had here, as everyone goes in for vegetables. Noony and
Lina have begun to cultivate their wonderful kitchen garden
and are waiting for our deaf-and-dumb friend to come with his
horses and plough up and harrow the soil before they can plant
anything.

You must have thought me crazy to ask you to bring me
so many things, but I did not realize at the time how difficult it
was to buy anything in England. How are you off for clothes
darling? Do you have to have elegant frocks? Here we do not
require to dress much, as there is no society. I am the only

person in this place who wears a hat. Everyone else wears a lakatins, which I hate. Old and young, all the same. I am still wearing a hat I bought in London ten years ago, and it is still admired and thought swanky. There is no competition you see.

Your fondly loving and adoring Mumsy

Oceans of love from Ganf and Noony.

Tuesday

Bulduri
May 7th 1946

My precious darling Rhona

Just a line to greet you on this frosty morning. Yesterday we had −1° of frost, and today −0° with brilliant sunshine. This must seem very odd to you, especially as these 'lines' will take at least two months to reach you. The trees and bushes have got green overnight, as they do in this funny climate, and hope of happy days to come fill our hearts.

Oh, how I wish you could see this room. I love it so, and with the morning sun streaming in through the five windows, it's lovely. I have a new pupil, who is most fascinating. She is a girl of twenty, very pretty and with the most charming manners. Her name is Irene. She was born in Paris, educated partly in France and partly in Rome; speaks beautiful French and Italian, besides Russian, German and Latvian and a smattering of English. She is very keen on English and we have arranged for two lessons a week: first an hour of English, and then an hour of Italian conversation and reading. You can't think what a joy it is to me, as, although I know *Toscano a fondo a fondo* and have been very successful in teaching it to many people, I have never had the opportunity of speaking the language; so I speak haltingly and grope for words, but I am sure that in a few months I shall be able to express myself quite fluently.

Irene lives at Pumpuri and actually walked all those miles for her first lesson, as she had promised to be here at eleven and there was no train. It took her two hours, I think. She lives with her grandmother who expects her to go to bed at eight pm. She goes to her job at seven am returns home at seven pm and has been in despair because she had no time and no chance of improving her mind. This has given her a new zest in life. Excuse my havering away like this, darling; but you will understand how happy it makes me to have such an interesting and unusual pupil. Besides it is so much easier for me to explain things in French than in Latvian. Though my Latvian pupils get on very well too.

111

I have three little girls of twelve who are marvels. Dagegen a boy of eleven, the brother of one of these 'marvels' is the most awful dunce I have ever come across. He can't tell the difference between f and h — and makes the same faults time after time and invariably spells *you*: ouy, and *your*: uory. He is hopeless, though a very well-behaved little fellow and quite unaware of his stupidity. *Basta*!

Noony is busy this morning, as usual, fetching immense sacks full of chips with which we light the stoves, the kitchen and the drawing room fireplace. They make glorious fires. She and Alide fetch on an average ten sacks a day, and the stable is half full of chips right up to the ceiling.

My love and a chaste kiss to Ches and tenderest love, hugs and kisses to your darling self

from Mumsy

Tuesday
Bulduri
14th May 1946

My darling darling Rhona

Our summer has not begun yet, and you would laugh if you could see me all wrapped up in shawls, with fox-fur mittens on my wrists and warm slippers on my feet. Noony has given me a pair of lovely crimson slippers made out of odds and ends of crimson plush out of Cariah's rag-bag, lined with flannel and trimmed with fur — *très chic*. We still have night frosts, and today it is damp and gloomy. I light a fire in the drawing room whenever I feel inclined, as Uni has an unlimited supply of chips which burn gloriously. She brings in eight or ten sacksful daily.

I spend quite a lot of time at my beloved piano. I am learning a Sonata of Beethoven, and know the first movement, eight pages off by heart, as well as parts of the two other movements; which is funny, because I have never been able to learn music by heart, not even when I was young. I think it is because my eyesight is bad now and I cannot see the notes, and so have to rely on my memory. Ganf goes down to the beach every afternoon. Unfortunately there are no seats there, or else he might sit and watch the sea and the sky, but he goes there and back in three quarters of an hour, comes back to tea and then we sit out and grill in the sun. Noony has been sleeping out on the balcony for quite a long time. She is indefatigable working in the garden from early morning till late at night. It is still daylight when we go to bed at ten-thirty. In between she makes many excursions to the saw-mill near the bridge, bringing home supplies of chips — on an average ten immense sacks a day. The stables are chock-full; we burn nothing else.

Your adoring Mumsy

Much love to Ches from us all. Ganf and Noony send you oceans of love and good wishes.

113

Tuesday

My adored darling Rhona

Did I tell you, or have you heard tell on the wireless that they
have started a steamer from London to Petersburg, presumably a passenger boat, which, provided you can obtain a visa,
might later on land you here? Ganf is willing to pay your return
passage from London hither. But we must not be too sangui-
nary (I don't mean bloody. I have an idea that it means too
hopeful). I hope, darling, your neuritis has been cured. I know
how painful it is. Massage is good for it, and I should say the
climate of Ecuador would cure it automatically. I trust you
have had no more earthquakes. That must have been a terrifying experience.

Today is just six months to Christmas. And how fast those
six months will fly past, and there we shall be again in cold and
darkness which I hate. I adore these long, light days, when I
rise early and enjoy a long morning with all my hobbies. The
room is lovely, with a huge bowl of yellow wild flowers which
look like a flaming fire — pink peonies — forget-me-nots, and a
tall vase of graceful spiraeas, like ostrich feathers, on the
piano.

On the 21st of June, being the longest day, I have always
made a practice of going down to the beach to see the sunset; I
crawled down on Friday, but for the last time. It is much too
far for me and I vowed I should never do it again. It was
agonies. The following day we went to the cemetery to put
some flowers on Cariah's grave, it being the anniversary of her
death. But that too was too much for me, though I rested at the
Irbes', half-way — at the station and again in the churchyard.
An elderly Russian couple, walking behind us said: old age is
coming on. When they had passed us they turned round and
asked how old I was. I said eighty-five, high time for me to
depart. And they said 'We thought you were seventy; Live
Granny, live.' Everybody asks me my age, soldiers and all. I
suppose it is a Russian custom. Though I am such an old
cripple, it's only my leg. Otherwise I am 'ale and 'earty and full
of haricots.

Tuesday

My own darling Curlylocks

We have been having lovely warm weather lately. For seven consecutive days I wrote 'brilliant' three times a day in Ganf's weather-book. But since Sunday it has turned chilly and showery — and though we are glad of the rain, so that Noony should have a rest from everlasting watering, unfortunately both she and Ganf have taken cold. Noony coughs and Ganf has a slight (I hope) attack of bronchitis. He still insists on going out for a little toddle every day — and I hope they will soon be better.

Lina goes nearly every day to the country to work for the one-eyed farmer. She walks there and back, seven kilometres each way when her bike is out of repair and arrived home at ten pm last night, having walked barefoot in torrents of rain, drenched to the skin — and popped straight into a hot bath. It had been frightfully hot and sultry and she was helping the farmer to collect the bees which had swarmed. 'Hot sun in back; black in eyes; I fall and don't know anything. (That is her way of describing a slight sun-stroke.) I wokes up. Father Bee on one knee looking at me with his one eye says "Are you better." I says "Better *is*" and I gots up, faded and sicks — and think I must go on with bees.'

There is no black market here, because you are allowed to buy or sell anything you like, only the prices are prohibitive. On Saturday we celebrated the 65th anniversary of Ganf's arrival in Riga, and Uni bought 100 gr cocoa and some white bread and surprised us with a delicious treat at teatime. Sitting in the garden we enjoyed it very much and made Ganf tell us all about his arrival and his first impressions.

Your fondly loving

Mumsy

Tuesday

Bulduri
July 16th 1946

My beloved darling Rhona

Slap, bang! here we are again. And jolly dogs are we! (Shakespeare). This is my twenty-first letter to you since February 5th. Am I not a good Mumsy, as regular as clockwork? It is eight am and there is an almighty thunderstorm going on, with hailstones and coals of fire, as the Psalmist describes it. The rain sweeps past in sheets, just like a blizzard, and obliterates the whole landscape. Ganf was so excited, he leapt out of bed to watch the storm. Then back to bed, with all the curtains drawn back, in order that he might see the dazzling flashes of lightning. Thank goodness the garden will not need watering for days, for indeed it is a labour.

Your loving Mumsy

Bulduri
July 30th 1946

My Treasure-Child!

Ganf's bronchitis is nearly gone — each attack leaves him thinner and more gaunt, poor darling. His temples are fallen in like those of an old horse. Otherwise he is just the same, always calm and sweet, and his mind as clear as ever. He will be eighty-seven on September 7th.

Rhona darling, it is very touching that you should be so homesick for your old home and the old folk; and I am very glad it was a happy home for you. But I cannot help thinking it must hurt Ches. I hope, my beloved child, you try to make his home (and yours) happy and bright. It is a wonderful thing to think that the wife is like a Queen in her home, with the power to make everybody happy, or profoundly miserable. Please don't be angry with me for giving you a 'pi jaw' — but I think it so important to realize how much depends on you. Do you decorate your rooms with flowers and make them all bright and *omutigs*? This room is my constant joy and delight, with masses of flowers — red and yellow shades predominating at the moment. I am so glad to hear you are taking an interest in gardening. It sure is an absorbing hobby, and one which grows on you. I think it is wonderful that you can grow pineapples and grapefruit, and that everything grows so quickly.

My gardening days, alas! are over, for though I can stoop for hours without feeling giddy, I cannot stand for five minutes, my legs are so painful. Yes, your Mumsy and Ganf are getting very old, and so you must make every effort to come and see them before it is too late. In case you have not had the letter I wrote you concerning your passage, I repeat that Ganf will gladly pay your fare from London to Riga and back.

Your adoring Mumsy

Darling child, you sure do say very flattering things about me; but I think you idealize me, and from brooding over your longing to see your old Mumsy again, you make me out quite a paragon, whereas I have no illusions about myself, and I know I am a very ordinary old woman, in fact as they say in Devonshire 'a proper old bitch I be.' I can't think what 'antics' of mine you have been telling your friends. I am not aware of having perpetrated any antics; you must have mixed me up with your paternal grandmother Cordelia Hall. And as for telling anyone the sad story of my flop-belly, that was very naughty of you — it was only meant for your private ear. I did not even think it necessary to say 'Don't tell Ches', being confident of your discretion. I don't know how I shall ever be able to look my great-grandson in the face if you have been taking away my character and inventing what you call 'antics' *à mon compte*, you wicked brat! There, now you have had your scolding; put it in your pipe and smoke it.

I have two new pupils, very intelligent ones whom it is a pleasure to teach. The Jew-boy is delightful, such a sense of humour he has. That brings my score up to twenty five hours a week = 100 hours a month. I have almost succeeded in taming the little Russian Tom Thumb who bites me, and kicks me and butts me in the tum with his head. He now has the option of a birch-rod or a sweet, and he usually chooses the latter. He was perfectly angelic today.

Poor Noony started off on her bike yesterday to pay our rent and other things, including the lawyer's fee — skidded and capsized, bike and all, and only when got to Dubbeln did she notice that she had lost her bag containing various documents, her passport, our ration cards for this month and 900 Rbls = £45. Of course when she retraced her steps it was gone, *Spurlos verschwunden.* A nice find for somebody. Don't allude to it when you write, as she might not like me to mention it.

Your loving Mumsy

My darling Treasure-Child

On Saturday was Ganf's birthday (eighty-seven). I gave him a pair of socks, and Mrs Foster A., Mrs Sparnin, and Olla Ellis each gave him cigarettes, the latter gave him 100! and Mr Mezit also sent him some. Besides that Mrs Sparnin gave him flowers and hot house grapes.

We have bought a young pig and are elevating it with a view to feeding you on pork chops. We call it Ruksit, and it has a very good appetite. We are now busy gathering peas, beans and broad beans to dry for the winter — and I think we shall have enough veg to see us till next season. Noony has a very good harvest of tomatoes, and besides eating them three times a day we are swopping them for manteca (or mantequilla if you prefer it) and carne. I wonder how you will like our food. There will always be quantities of potatoes for you to fill up the corners with. We enjoy all our meals. We had roast pava, a tiny one on Ganf's birthday.

Our summer is on its last legs, and we are being blest with thunderstorms and cloud-bursts. Still Ganf trots out twice a day. I seldom go out because of my lameness. I can walk fairly well with the aid of two sticks, but that looks so silly. My mornings are mostly free now, but my afternoons are very busy, because all the children who go to school can only come *por la tarde.*

God bless you my angel.
Gruss! Kuss! Schluss!

Mummy

My unspeakably beloved Rhona

Poor darling Ganf tripped over a root yesterday and came down a cropper and bruised his forehead and nose, and I expect he will have a black eye today. As for me I am suffering from swelled head because of all the flattering things you say of me, my darling. My brain reels under the strong, unaccustomed words of praise. I forget that I have not earned it. Your words of admiration fall like the blade of knighthood on my cowering shoulders, and I arise from my knees and stand erect, feeling as though I had gained in stature. While, as a matter of fact I am shrinking every day owing to the progress of arthritis deformans; and whenever I pass a mirror I think 'This is none of Oi', like the old woman whose petticoats had been cut shorter while she slept.

Lina went to see some friends in town one day and she saw two white coffins being carried into a flat in their house. She was told that they were destined for a girl of eighteen and a young man of twenty-one. They were engaged to be married, and he had to go back to Moscow — and as she refused to accompany him thither, he shot her dead and then shot himself. Lina went to her friends again on Saturday and was told that the bodies had been taken to the cemetery, where they were received by two orthodox priests. The coffins were deposited on the ground, the lids were removed and the corpses exposed to view. He was in evening dress, and she was arrayed as a bride with a veil, and wreath and all. The first priest united them, the young couple, in holy matrimony, after which they were lowered into one grave and the second priest read the burial service over them. Quaint, *n'est-ce pas?*

My love

It is three months today till Christmas Eve. Will my little love be here by then, looking at our tiny tree and talking of past Christmases and of all that has happened since then? She will have much to tell her old Mumsy, and Ganf and Noony who will listen greedily to all she has to say. I am looking forward to your teaching me Spanish.

This morning I overslept myself and did not awake till nine, having been kept awake from eleven till five am by an infernal flea (the first, and I hope the last, of the season) careering round and round my neck till I was nearly crazy, singing

There's a fascination frantic
In a ruin that's romantic

and imagining, silly fool, that it was Airborne, winning the Derby. I couldn't catch the brute, because the electric light in our bedroom has gone phutt.

My own, own darling Treasure-Child

I often try to picture to myself the arrival of my Treasure-Child. Seated at my writing-table I suddenly look up and behold a vision of beauty standing in the doorway: my Curly-locks, her eyes shining, her face flushed with running all the way from the station in the crisp, frosty air. Senile tears from rheumy eyes course down my pendulous cheeks and form a little pool on the blue carpet. With a cry of joy I struggle to my feet, grasp my two walking-sticks and hasten to meet her. Spreading out my arms in order to clasp her to my able-bodied buzzim, I drop my styx and perform a sentada into the pool of tears. Here I must burst into French, partly because it sounds more elegant, partly for the benefit of the censor who is wondering what this is all about — for I am sure he understands French much better than English. All Russians do. *Tout le monde se precipite pour me soulever, mais moi je les écarte tous, et je me releve fort gracieusement.* I then embrace my darling child and cuddle her to suffocation. How does that strike you for a meeting? Or is your forecast different?

Poor darling Ganf is still a semi-invalid. He stays in bed till one pm and then sits in the little room till six or seven, looking very frail and depressed. How it would cheer him up to see you! How we both long to make dear Ches's acquaintance. It is only natural to want to meet the fox who has stolen away our gosling.

My own darling, little Rhona

This letter is to convey to you all our most heartfelt wishes to
you for many, many happy, happy returns of November 11th.
I am afraid it will be late, but we shall be thinking of you on
that day and drinking your health in cocoa.

We have harvested our potatoes, a goodly supply, and
collected the last of the beans and other vegetables, and the
whole kitchen-garden has been ploughed up, ready for next
spring. The dining room and even the morning room are
decorated with strings of tobacco-leaves which are drying. The
hay-loft is quite full too, and every evening Noony toils at the
leaves, stringing them on wire — quite a labour. She is never
idle for one moment. Today she has gone off to Belten again
for onions and what not. Ganf has made a good recovery, and
has resumed his daily walks. We have −2° of frost today and it
is snowing and Noony has fetched five sacks of chips in her
hand-sledge.

Ganf has developed an extraordinary thirst for the last
two or three weeks. He drinks water all day long, and I get up
three times in the night to fill his glass and his cup. We have
tried to get a bottle of cognac as a pick-me-up for him at bedtime; but there is none to be had, nor whisky nor nothing. My
Treasure-Child, though I did not bring you up on ultra early-
Victorian lines as I was dragged up myself, yet I never allowed
you to contradict me, now will I allow you to do so now. You
have just *got* to let Ganf pay your fare from London hither
(return). It will make your journey cheaper and the pleasure of
meeting will be ours as well as yours. So, *basta*!

I am looking forward to playing a little game of cards with
you that I have adapted from a patience. We shall play for one
Rouble points. I used to play it with Cariah, and now I play it
with her once in the morning and once in the evening, lest she
should feel lonesome in her tomb. You will have to look after
your luggage 'cos the place is teeming with pickpockets of the

123

deepest dye. My beloved darling child, I know our prayers will be answered and you will be allowed to come and see those who love you so dearly and are so grateful to God for your love and devotion. But be prepared to be disillusioned, because the place is so changed as to be unrecognizable, and your old parents are just two old crocks. Seven years make such a difference at our age. Give my love and two kisses to Ches.

All my love embraces and hugs to your darling self.

Your own adoring Mumsy

Bulduri
October 30th 1946

My darling darling Rouite

By now you will have heard the dreadful news that our one and only precious Mum has gone from us. I wired Madgie to tell you by letter as a wire would have been such a terrible shock to you. Darling it just doesn't bear thinking about and I know what a crushing blow it is to you who have thought and hoped and longed so much to be with her again — but be brave about it for that is what she would wish and though Fate has decreed that you are not to see her in this world — you know she is still with you and always will be — I *know* and feel intensely that she hasn't left us and she will *always* be with her loved ones. It will be an everlasting comfort to you to know how happy you made her by writing such sweet loving letters — she looked forward to them so eagerly and read them till she knew them by heart and wept with happiness at the loving things you wrote. She was so happy to know that you loved her so, and it is too too tragic that you were not able to be with her again. She was so looking forward to your coming and we talked of it such a lot — if only you had been able to come last year! Oh, it just doesn't bear thinking about.

We mustn't regret darlingest we must be very thankful that she was spared a long and painful illness or any ordinary sort of stroke that would have caused her to lie unable to move or speak.

Darling Mumsy was her old self almost to the very end and it is given to few to be so bright mentally at her age. On Tuesday evening (October 22nd) she got up from the sofa to walk the few steps to the table for supper and as she reached the edge of the table she said 'I can't move my right leg,' so I helped her into her chair and she sat down looking very pale — then she said 'I don't know what has happened to me I can't speak properly' — and it sounded as if she had a big potato in her mouth. It only lasted a few moments and I sort of didn't let her see I noticed anything and passed it off — but it gave me an awful turn for I knew it was a slight stroke. She was all right but didn't make a very good supper and we all went to bed early — I gave her some of Ganf's heart medicine — a sort of

125

pick me up and suggested she should stay in bed next morning. However she was up at the usual time and said she felt OK, had her pupils, played the piano and read to Ganf and she and I played several games of chess as usual — her appetite was good; the following day (Thursday) she seemed again her old self — though in the afternoon she said she felt cold; at supper she said — 'if I tell you something will you promise me two things' — I hesitated and said I'll see and then said OK. She said I've got a bad sore throat, promise you won't send for the doctor — promise not to keep me in bed. She ate very little supper and found difficulty in swallowing. I made her a hot camomile compress and gave her warm camomile to gargle with — her temperature was 38.5°. Next morning her throat was so bad she could scarcely speak so I went for the doctor and he diagnosed acute laryngitis — afterwards I told him about the little stroke and he said 'that makes it quite a different matter' and altered his prescriptions.

She was unable to swallow more than an occasional spoonful of milk and honey during the day and when I took her temp in the evening it was 43° and more if the thermometer had registered more. Lina went for the doctor at six-thirty am and he said he could do nothing — the nurse came and gave her an injection and she went to sleep and her breathing gradually became easier and less of a choke and by the afternoon she was breathing more naturally — but she never opened her eyes again — she left us at five pm on Saturday October 26th. She looked so sweet — so young and peaceful — I wish and I wish you could have seen her. Poor darling Mums it seems quite incredible that she is no longer with us. Poor Ganf — it was an awful blow — he said 'I did think I would go first.' Darling Rhona I can't tell you how sorry I am for you — dear Ches will help you to bear the blow and darling I know I could never replace the only Mum that ever was but I will try if you will let me and we will comfort each other by letter till we can meet. I will tell you about the funeral tomorrow. All my love and sympathy darling and bear up and be brave as Mum would have you be.

Your own

Noons

Darlingest Rouite

I wanted to write you immediately after the funeral but there has been so much to do and write and I still feel all in a dream or rather nightmare and can't sort of gather my thoughts together — I feel as if I had a brick in my head instead of a brain — you will understand darling and forgive me; the bottom has fallen out of our little world and there is nothing but emptiness.

The funeral was lovely and if only you had been there you would have been comforted and happy to think that darling Mum was laid to rest with so much love from all who knew and adored her. Mum looked so sweet and young lying in her coffin — she looked really *happy*. The coffin stood on a bier draped with the Legation flag (which is in my keeping) and surrounded by palms and greenery brought by neighbours — and tall candles. I put a Union Jack in the coffin — an eider-down on that and then the sheet — the coffin lid was draped with another Union Jack and was buried like that, so that she lies on and under the Flag she so loved. The few remaining British came from town and all our farm friends from over the river — one of them provided a trap for Ganf and the parson and another a horse and cart for a hearse — the local people all came so that the crowd was huge.

The old clergyman who married Lorna and buried Dad has left and so rather than have a stranger we asked our dear old Russian Priest to officiate, Mum liked him. We had the funeral service at the house so that it should be short for Ganf at the cemetery — the drawing room was packed and heaped up with wreaths and flowers — it was a dull and gloomy day but as darling Mum was carried out and the procession started the sun came out and remained out till all was over and then vanished as suddenly as it appeared.

I wish you could have seen the grave — a veritable hill of flowers, her pupils — the school children clubbed together for a lovely wreath and they were all howling as if it was their own

127

mother who had gone. Rouite, *you* will know what it was to come back to the empty house — it is no good talking about it and darling I feel for you more than I can say for I know how desperately hard it is for you that you could not have come in time and have not been able to see her again. I have all these years to be thankful for and have had the happiness of being with her to the last. Of course one knew that the parting would have to come some day but she could have lived to be a hundred she was so full of life and one never even thought of her passing on so soon.

Noons

Bulduri
November 11th 1946

Darling Rouite

We are thinking of you on this your birthday — we would have sent you a wire had things been different but you understand darling that the bottom having fallen out of our little world one has not heart for anything. Darling Mum was such a very special sort of person it takes a lot more getting used to not having her with us — in fact I wonder if we ever shall, she has left a gap that nothing can ever fill.

Poor old Ganf is a bit better — he was so very shrunk and tired-looking but now thank goodness he seems to be picking up — he sleeps an awful lot but that is due to the diabetes and insulin injections; twice I have found him in floods of tears poor darling — when some tune that Mum loved was played on the wireless — then we both have a good howl and I think it does him good. We still have very mild weather and the masses of flowers on Mum's grave are still fresh and untouched by frost. Darling Rouite I wish you were here with us — will you still try to come?

I have just come back from the cemetery — I go every day — and it really was wonderful there, so quiet and peaceful, lovely sunshine and all Mum's wreaths and flowers covered with hoar frost so that they looked as if they had just come out of the greenhouse. The trees were full of bullfinches and woodpeckers and tomtits, a squirrel was chewing cones half-way up a tree and a dear little mouse, dark yellow with a black stripe down the middle of its back was running about in and out of the wreaths looking for I don't know what — it was perfectly sweet and didn't take the slightest notice of me. There was a feeling of happiness in the place and I could have sat there for hours only it was very cold, −12° and an east wind and that temperature when there is no snow on the ground is bitter. It is three weeks since Mum was laid to rest there and it still seems like a dream and I expect to see Mum sitting in her chair as

129

usual when I come into the room. Of course one doesn't realize she was nearly eighty-six and that few people attain that age though our families seem to be exceptional — both my grandmother were over eighty-five and all Ganf's sisters have passed that age.

Ganf is keeping fairly well though he is suffering from breathlessness as he always does in winter — it must be dreadful for him to be able to do nothing but just sit and think — I read to him but we have no books that really interest him — I don't know what he would do without the wireless for he really enjoys music; I think I told you I had got him a little loudspeaker for his bedroom and switch it on when there is anything good after he has gone to bed — last night we had the Pathétique and he enjoyed it very much. Can you get all stations and do you get good programmes or do you have to listen to the rotten stuff the Yanks call 'music'. Sorry this is such a dull letter darling but it brings all my love to you and Ches and a special hug from your own old

Noons.

Ganf sends you his very best love darling.

Bulduri
November 26th 1946

Darling Rouite

I wrote to you five days ago, my fourth letter since darling
Mums left us just a month ago today and now I must tell you
that darling Ganf is on his way to join her. He had the same
kind of attack that he has had several times before — failure of
the heart to pump up sufficient blood to the brain — on Saturday he collapsed in the bathroom and sat on a chair trying to
get his breath and yawning — I stood beside him nearly an
hour to prevent his falling off the chair and eventually Lina
came along and with the postman's help we carried him to bed
and there he has lain ever since quietly sinking — the doctor
says all the works are just worn out and it won't be very long
before he fades away in his sleep. Mum's going so suddenly
was too much of a shock for him — he just didn't want to live
and got completely apathetic — the diabetes too weakened
him. I sleep in Mum's bed so as to be at hand to give him a
drink and he talks a lot in his sleep and keeps calling out
'Pooney' poor darling. I am afraid you will get the news that he
has left us from Madgie long before this reaches you — it is
dreadfully sad that you couldn't see them again — they did so
long for you to come — but such is life with its sorrows and dis-
appointments which just can't be helped.

  After Mum's funeral the farm friend whose horse pulled
the hearse said 'I shan't say goodbye because in a very short
time I shall be here with my horse for the next funeral' — I
asked what she meant and she said — 'as the coffin was lifted
onto the cart the horse dropped its card — that means another
funeral — as I go in to drive home it did it again — that means
very soon.' Curious superstition and apparently it comes true.
Well darling no more now and don't be too sad — life is like
that only we kidded ourselves that Mum and Ganf were
immortal and didn't realize that they were so old — we are
very lucky that they have been spared to us so long.

                                        Love and hugs
                                        Noons

Darlingest Rouite

Yesterday poor old Ganf was laid to rest in the same grave as Mum — 'in death they were not divided'. I am very happy to think of that — Ganf just didn't want to live without her and, as the doctor said — all the works were run down and he just faded away poor darling. As I wrote you last week (27th) he seemed exhausted — just tired — and slept nearly all the time. I slept in Mum's bed and was in and out of bed every half hour to give him a drink etc and the last two nights I slept on chairs beside his bed as he was talking so indistinctly I couldn't hear what he wanted unless close up — he spoke little, even that was an effort, and four-fifteen on Thursday morning 28th he just quietly passed on. It is dreadfully sad to lose them both so suddenly and I am desperately sorry for you darling — after all your efforts to get home — nothing but emptiness and a hopeless feeling.

Ganf's funeral was exactly like Mum's — the same floral decorations provided by kind neighbours — a similar coffin, covered with a Union Jack which was buried too and the same crowd of people — the same weather — very mild and gloomy — clearing up as the procession started, the same old parson and masses of flowers. Mum's wreaths were quite fresh still and the joint grave is a wonderful sight.

Only one thing was different and it is rather curious: just before Mum's funeral Ganf asked me what horse was going to pull her coffin — I told him it was a horse offered by a farm friend — 'Yes', he said, 'but I mean what colour.' 'White,' I said. 'Oh,' says Ganfs, 'in my dream I saw a brown horse pulling the coffin.' Well when he died I asked the same friend for her white horse and she promised to come but on the morning of the funeral she sent to say she was prevented from coming and had asked her neighbour to come with his horse and he came with a *brown* one!

It was dreadful coming back to the empty house and I sort

of feel what's the good of anything — all the fuel I collected to keep them warm — cellar full of spuds and vegs, the pig ready for slaughter — the fowls and pounds and pounds of baccy — there's no object in anything any more!

> Tons of love and hugs darling
> from your sorrowful old
> Noons
>
> Love to Ches.

AT THEIR DEPARTING
A Childhood Memoir
Nancy Thompson

Armistice Day 1918. Grey, bleak Middlesbrough, haunted by
unemployment, poverty and the grim war years, put on its
Sunday best and danced and sang — a revelation to one
three-and-a-half year old observer for whom life was just
beginning. Nancy Thompson's vivid memoir recalls the
pleasures and dramas of childhood: the excitement of learning
to read; the wonder of music; a magical visit to cousin Liz at
Huck-a-Back far away on the moors; the traumatic trip to the
seaside when sister Bessie almost drowned. Each treasured
episode conveys a fresh awareness of life and death and the
fearful, inevitable growing-up.

Through a child's acute vision there emerges a picture of life
in the North East that is deeply moving and quite
unforgettable.

'A really wonderful account of a working class childhood,
rich in detail, vivid in presentation, and absorbing from
beginning to end. A real pleasure'
ALAN SILLITOE

'Fascinating . . . a valuable collection of memories of northern
life after the First World War'
TIMES EDUCATIONAL SUPPLEMENT

'The past is astonishingly alive to this accomplished author'
YORKSHIRE LIFE

FUTURA PUBLICATIONS
NON-FICTION/AUTOBIOGRAPHY
0 7088 3251 2

ONE FAMILY'S WAR
Edited by Patrick Mayhew

In 1939, Lady Mayhew decided that her war-splintered family
should channel letters through her, to be typed and
distributed. Without this intimate bulletin, the six young
Mayhews and two first cousins, the Howarths, serving in the
Army, the Navy, the RAF, Special Operations Executive, the
Field Auxiliary Nursing Yeomanry, the Wrens, the Home Guard
and the Auxiliary Fire Service, would soon have lost touch.
Beryl wrote in every newsletter from Felthorpe Hall, the family
home then acting as a receiving home for expectant mothers,
and reproduced the precious news from loved ones in Egypt,
New York, Tunisia, Sicily, and the killing fields of Europe.

ONE FAMILY'S WAR records an English family's wide-ranging
experiences under the stress of war in a rich kaleidoscope of
correspondence.

'Fascinating correspondence . . . I urge that it should be read'
Beryl Bainbridge, TIMES LITERARY SUPPLEMENT

'Remarkable . . . deserves mention beside Evelyn Waugh's
PUT OUT MORE FLAGS'
David Holloway, DAILY TELEGRAPH

'More vivid than any history'
MAIL ON SUNDAY

FUTURA PUBLICATIONS
NON-FICTION/BIOGRAPHY
0 7088 2907 4

MAD WHITE GIANT
Benedict Allen

Benedict Allen's passion for the South American jungle grew
from romantic tales which impressed him as a schoolboy,
until, at 23, undaunted by warnings from friends, travellers
and members of the august Royal Geographical Society,
dreams gave way to reality, a 700-mile expedition from the
Orinoco to the mouth of the Amazon.

Travelling on foot (blistered and bitten) and by canoe (braving
rapids and a truculent crew), he survived on stewed monkey,
locusts and berries; learned how to handle a Winchester
from a Sicilian; resisted the advances of lovely Zorola of the
Orinoco delta; and was led by sceptical Indians deep into the
jungle. There he wrestled gloriously with a wild pig to win
honour amongst the Wai-wai and to be rewarded with the
offer of marriage to seductive Yimshi, true acceptance by her
people. The Indians named him Louco Benedito — Mad
White Giant. Only later came betrayal by guides in the grip
of gold fever . . .

'Marvellous descriptions of the horrors and beauty of the
jungle, the infernal racket, the fat mangoes festooned with
orchids, and a strong Boy's Own element of treachery versus
loyalty'
LONDON STANDARD

FUTURA PUBLICATIONS
NON-FICTION
0 7088 3053 6

TOBO
One Woman's Escape
Jane Tierney

'An amazing adventure'
MAIL ON SUNDAY

Aged 19 and just married to a dashing RAF squadron leader, a determined Jane Tierney followed her husband to a Singapore posting and a life of colonial ease. Then the Japanese attacked Malaya. Morgan, gravely wounded on a daredevil mission, was admitted to the last hospital ship to leave; but Jane was too late. Captured by the Japanese, she was interned in a Java prison camp.

Scarred by torture and humiliation, Jane drew on her remaining strength and her tenacious love of life to escape, against all odds. Close to starvation and despair, she survived a gruelling trek across Java to join other civilians and Service personnel bound for Australia on an ancient Chinese river boat. Only to learn that Morgan's ship had been sunk . . .

TOBO — one woman's incredible experience, a real life TENKO.

FUTURA PUBLICATIONS
NON-FICTION/AUTOBIOGRAPHY
0 7088 3046 3

AN INDIAN ATTACHMENT
Sarah Lloyd

Sarah Lloyd spent two years in India with a young Sikh, first
in a remote Punjab village and then in the primitive community
of a 'holy man'. When she first saw Jungli in the steaming
heat of Calcutta she was captivated by his simplicity, his
spontaneity, his unselfishness. Two months later she felt
compelled to find him. So began their strange, turbulent and
ultimately doomed love affair. She an educated Westerner;
he an unemancipated, non-English speaking enigma, fiercely,
hopelessly in love with her, drawing her daily closer to the
rhythms of his life — with its stark surroundings and harsh
climate, its hardships and its simple pleasures. Until they finally
realised they must part.

'A traveller's tale, a love story, a brilliant exposé of village
India . . . a remarkable book'
SUNDAY TELEGRAPH

'Serious, honest, rare and extraordinary'
FINANCIAL TIMES

'Travel writing will never be the same again'
STANDARD

FUTURA PUBLICATIONS
NON-FICTION
0 7088 2683 0

All Futura Books are available at your bookshop or
newsagent, or can be ordered from the following address:
Futura Books, Cash Sales Department,
P.O. Box 11, Falmouth, Cornwall, TR10 9EN.

Please send cheque or postal order (no currency), and
allow 60p for postage and packing for the first book plus
25p for the second book and 15p for each additional book
ordered up to a maximum charge of £1.90 in U.K.

B.F.P.O. customers please allow 60p for the first book,
25p for the second book plus 15p per copy for the next
7 books, thereafter 9p per book.

Overseas customers, including Eire, please allow £1.25
for postage and packing for the first book, 75p for the second
book and 28p for each subsequent title ordered.